THE
RECKONING

Also by Randall Robinson

THE DEBT
DEFENDING THE SPIRIT

THE
RECKONING

WHAT BLACKS OWE
TO EACH OTHER

RANDALL
ROBINSON

DUTTON

DUTTON
Published by the Penguin Group
Penguin Putnam Inc., 375 Hudson Street, New York, New York 10014, U.S.A.
Penguin Books Ltd, 80 Strand, London WC2R 0RL, England
Penguin Books Australia Ltd, Ringwood, Victoria, Australia
Penguin Books Canada Ltd, 10 Alcorn Avenue, Toronto, Ontario, Canada M4V 3B2
Penguin Books (N.Z.) Ltd, 182–190 Wairau Road, Auckland 10, New Zealand

Penguin Books Ltd, Registered Offices: Harmondsworth, Middlesex, England

First published by Dutton, a member of Penguin Putnam Inc.

First printing, January 2002
1   3   5   7   9   10   8   6   4   2
Copyright © Randall Robinson, 2002
All rights reserved

LIBRARY OF CONGRESS CATALOGING-IN-PUBLICATION DATA
Robinson, Randall.
The reckoning : what Blacks owe to each other / Randall Robinson.
p. cm.
Includes index.
ISBN 0-525-94625-X (alk. paper)
1. African Americans—Social conditions—1975– 2. African American youth—Social
conditions. 3. African Americans—Economic conditions. 4. African American
youth—Economic conditions. 5. Inner cities—United States. 6. United States—
Social conditions—1980– 7. Social classes—United States. 8. Social ethics—United
States. 9. United States—Race relations. I. Title.

E185.86 .R73 2002
305.896'073—dc21
2001046029

Printed in the United States of America

Again, for Hazel

CONTENTS

Contents

THE
RECKONING

INTRODUCTION

The story that is the centerpiece of this book is true. The names of its principal characters, Peewee Kirkland, New Child Lynch, and Mark Lawrence, are real. I have changed the names of others for reasons that will become obvious.

I do not venture in this telling far afield of the events of the lives remarked here. You, no doubt, would have puzzled out the reasons for this narrowness of compass on your own. Sometimes, very old, very broad stories are best told *small*, in consumable units of observed lives, replete with travail and stunted prospect. Social data, the scholar's tool, serve well enough in conveying the trend and breadth of social conditions. But the usefulness of the academician's bar graph ends there, bleaching from general view the searing pain and hopelessness borne by the modern, uncomprehending victims of old, obscure, and oft-transmuted American social policies. To understand the full damage that America has done to the black world over the last 346 years, we must extrapolate the general from the specific, not the other way around.

The young black men whose stories are told here represent the gravely endangered generation of the fathers of our future.

They, like the millions who comprise their peer ranks, were born into the rigged game of dysfunctional families, variably crippling poverty, poor education, and all but nonexistent opportunity for long-term success.

Some of them miraculously survive; a few, even, like Mark Lawrence and Peewee Kirkland, with an abiding exercise of fatherlike duty towards the many like New Child Lynch who are forced to contend with social obstacles that no child in a "civilized" society should ever be compelled to confront.

Such are the legacies for American blacks after 246 years of slavery and the century of government-embraced racial discrimination that followed on slavery's heels. One hundred and thirty-eight years after the Emancipation Proclamation, our young men, slavery's grandsons, are six times more likely to be arrested for a serious crime than are their white counterparts. After arrest, they are more likely than their white counterparts to be prosecuted and convicted. Upon conviction, they serve prison sentences roughly twice as long as those served by whites for the same crimes.

From birth, black inner-city males are strapped onto a hard-life treadmill leading all too often toward early death or jail. While the United States has the highest incarceration rate of any nation in the world, Washington, D.C., the nation's capital, has one of the highest in America. More than one in every three black men in the District of Columbia between the ages of eighteen and thirty-five falls under one or another arm of the criminal justice system.

Prisons, increasingly under private ownership, are a growth industry. Nothing inflates prison stock prices like the growing ranks of American prisoners, the majority of whom are being held for nonviolent crimes and, all too many, in places like Washington, D.C., well past the times set by the courts.

Public funds are being used to subsidize a national private prison industry whose growth depends on higher incarceration rates. Said differently, society is subsidizing its own demise for the benefit of private investors. The investors are disproportionately white. The prisoners are disproportionately black. Inside the new private hells, prisoners toil for private companies, earning but a pittance while undercutting the wages of non-prison labor. Owing to the extremely low wages for prison labor, the companies that employ prisoners constitute, not surprisingly, still another new growth industry. Towards this modern bondage, down this human cattle chute, black males from birth are being herded willy-nilly before our very eyes. It is this new de facto slavery that benefits the same private interests, transmogrified, that its predecessor institution benefited centuries before.

In my last book, *The Debt: What America Owes to Blacks*, I argued that only massive American government reparations can begin to repair the devastating economic and psychosocial injury done to blacks in America since 1619 at the hands of, first, the colonial governments, and, later, the American government. But while broad programmatic restitution can insure for African-Americans a future, it cannot salvage a living generation of African-American men and women who are being, in alarming numbers, lost to the black community as wives, husbands, mothers, fathers, breadwinners, and responsible social contributors.

This, we must do for ourselves.

May 1, 2001

1

THE LUNCHEON

A tiger, when attacked, fights alone. Even when the imperiled tiger is surrounded by fellow tigers, the tigers that are not in imminent danger do nothing to help. Lions defend against attack as a pride. No tiger attacks a lion within sight of another lion. A single lion, however, had it the will to, could slaughter every tiger on the planet, lined up cheek to jowl, one at a time.

The amplified voice I am sickest of hearing is my own. I don't know how the professional oracles do it, flooding the airways with their relentless blather.

Click.

. . . *let's get America moving again* . . .

Click.

. . . *the veterans have to step up their play* . . .

Click.

. . . *and Jaysus said* . . .

Click.

. . . *those Republicans will bust a hole in the deficit* (which was what I thought was the idea) . . .

Click. Tube Black.

God.

Killing speech with freedom. Killing freedom with speech. Spewed over a hundred channels, a thousand radio bands, countless big-talk conferences and small-talk panels, rubber-chicken luncheons and black-tie dinners. Inane, cacophonous talk. Millions of voices, aloft in the new technology's crowded sky of social issues entertainment. The voices detach from their owners and replicate disembodied, floating off into the economy as electronic units of the gross domestic product before homing onto a defenseless huddle of jaded listeners that include, justly, the voices' owners.

Click.

It is a Saturday in fall 1999. I turn off the talk station on my car radio and park in front of the Ira Aldridge Theater on the campus of Howard University in Washington, D.C. I am gripped with the mild depression that precedes every speech that I give. I am unprepared, but that is not the source of my despondence. I will give my LEGO talk, patched together extemporaneously from the thousands of speeches I have made before. Audiences seem to like this more than anything new that I could think of to say.

Now I know that this is a part of what depresses me. I am giving a *performance*. I will believe the words. But I have said the same words in the same order too many times. I am nearly always the *same*. Although the audiences may not seem the same, they can all be located on a curve the distance of which I have traveled back and again many times. Nothing is new. I am a commodity in democracy's mouthy comedic charade. Praise be to mammon, the powerless are allowed to talk. Indeed, we are encouraged to yammer futilely at the tops of our voices.

Days before having the good fortune of finding this parking

space on Howard's campus, my wife, Hazel, and I had gone to the Cuban Interests Section in Washington, D.C., to meet for an hour with Juan Miguel Gonzáles, who was in the country trying to retrieve his six-year-old son from his great-uncle Lazaro Gonzáles. Lazaro, egged on by thousands of Miami's self-exiled Castro-hating Cubans, had had custody of Elián for the five months since the boy was plucked from the sea in which his mother, her boyfriend, and others had perished. Although there is no evidence that Juan Miguel is anything but a fit father, Lazaro refuses to return his son to him, even in defiance of orders to do so from the Immigration and Naturalization Service, the U.S. Department of Justice, and a federal court. The Miami Cuban community, strengthened over the years by assistance from the federal government, seems now to have become a de facto government in exile under which some four hundred thousand *African-Americans* are constrained to live.

In this imbroglio over the fate of little Elián, the Miami Cubans have defined themselves less as Americans than as Cubans. Perhaps all of this had been made clear years ago when a bumper sticker had begun to appear with the legend *Will the last American leaving Miami please bring the flag.* In fact, Anglos *had* left Miami, and in droves, selling their property to the in-rushing Cubans. African-Americans and Haitians had been stuck. They had chafed under what appeared to them to be a provisional government of the New Cuban Republic of Miami.

The treatment of blacks in the New Cuba had disturbingly resembled that meted out to blacks in Cuba in the years before Castro. In those years Cuba had been racially segregated. The children, grandchildren, and great-grandchildren of those who had segregated Cuba were now in control of Miami, a Miami that was brazenly defying its erstwhile ally, the U.S. government.

Anyhow, where was I? I am thinking too much. I am nearly always involved in some exercise of counterproductive introspection. It could be that I am merely flattering myself. That I am tricking myself. That *introspection* is too high-sounding a word for what bothers me. Perhaps it is merely ego. I have accomplished a measure of prestige and material comfort. But I have no power. Perhaps, not even influence. Could it be that I have at last succumbed in retreat to the debilitating condition of careerism like all the rest? The talking heads. The *experts*. The media bees. The ambition junkies. The spin people. The celebrity liars. I do not *want* to make this speech. I do not want to get out of the car.

I have never had much talent for doing things in which I have little or no interest. My high school organic chemistry grade is early evidence of this trait. Perhaps this malaise with which I seem afflicted stems from a creeping involuntary likening of my career in human rights advocacy to playing the stock market, where the gains and losses seem as ephemeral as the paper on which they are reported. Distant. Remote. Manipulated. Undeserved. The real beneficiaries and victims seldom met, never known.

In the large public electronic forum of *Debate America* we have pretty much commodified, dehumanized, cartoonized, everything: issues, tactics, victims, victimizers, pain. Professional antagonists spar self-righteously in comfort above the fray of the affected like colliding noisy air masses. And then we careerists, left to right, accord *ourselves* badges of courage, devaluing both the very meaning of courage and the unsung anonymous who manifest it routinely.

Ours is a society in which the actor is more important than the real-life hero the actor portrays. I read somewhere that the

Scottish when erecting a statue in honor of the fabled guardian of Scotland, William Wallace, used not the likeness of Wallace, the real Braveheart, but that of the actor Mel Gibson. John Wayne, the Duke, takes pains to avoid the draft during World War II, before making himself into a war hero on film. Sport announcers tell us that the athlete who takes risks in a *game* has guts. Chris Matthews names his little TV talkfest *Hardball*. Basketball coach Bobby Knight, after choking one of his young Indiana University charges, waxes manly explaining that basketball isn't canasta.

I played basketball in college. Seen against a world in conflict, if basketball isn't canasta, it ain't much more. Guts are what honest judges in Colombia and community patrols in American inner cities have, not actors or basketball players or talk show hosts or American policy advocates for that matter.

Click.

It is midmorning and ugly. The rain falls in sheets and washes the creases from my trousers before I reach the venue of my luncheon speech. I pause in the lee of the building and struggle with my umbrella against the wind. Completing the task, I stand there. I take a deep breath. I do not know my hosts and I know almost nothing about their organization, the Black Male Empowerment Summit. The letter of invitation had been signed by a Mark Lawrence. Lawrence had described the mission of his organization as the salvage of endangered young black males and the empowerment of black men generally. Conferences, he said, were being held in major cities across the country to increase support for the organization's programs. He had written that the organization could offer only a token honorarium. I had accepted. As is always the case when faced with the reality of *giving* the speech, I wished I had not.

* * *

Howard's Blackburn Center is a modern, featureless contest between taste and budget. The large foyer has a slate-gray floor, a two-story ceiling, and a wallwide window that gives onto a picturesque pond with grassy, steeply sloping banks. I walk into the foyer and hesitate, waiting for someone to recognize me and direct me toward the banquet room in which I am to make my presentation.

"Good morning, Mr. Robinson. We're so glad you could be with us today." The well-dressed, thirtyish man had given his name, but I hadn't gotten it. I seem never to. In any case I confess that it is mildly, albeit stupidly, flattering to be recognized. Just the other day upon my approach with Hazel to the Cuban Interests Section for a visit with Juan Miguel Gonzáles, a white man, one of a large cluster of camera-laden journalists said to me, "Good morning, Reverend Jackson." This puts me in mind of a story the real Reverend Jackson told me. Sometime back when he was running for president and was featured on the cover of virtually every national newsmagazine, he had emerged from his New York hotel having had lunch with Zimbabwe's President Robert Mugabe before rushing off to other high-level meetings at the United Nations. He had, in those moments, been pridefully aware of his metamorphosis from impoverished South Carolina child to global celebrity.

In the lobby of the hotel, the Reverend Jackson's eyes found the beaming face of an elderly white woman. Magnanimously, he returned the approaching old woman's smile. Pressed for time, he managed a gracious patience as the old woman struggled to say her piece: "I really couldn't leave without thanking you for all that you have done."

Jackson was buoyed: *Even this old woman thinks I have made an important contribution to the world.*

Moving away, the old woman pressed a dollar into the Reverend Jackson's hand: "I never would have been able to lift these heavy bags. Thanks again and here's a little something for you."

"Good morning, Mr. Robinson. My name is Mark Lawrence. I am glad you could be with us." I have never known how to describe faces in a way that would tell you anything that you really need to know. And only in the rarest instances have I been able to form face pictures from the language of writers that I have read. A great many black men are Mark Lawrence's age (fortyish), height (six-two-ish), weight (one-seventy-ish), and complexion (a reddish medium brown) that hints of a childhood of freckles and umber-red hair that is decidedly different (much darker) than white people's red hair. But Mark Lawrence, who extends his hand, has no hair. His head, like mine, is shaved. His eyeglasses are nearly rimless and comport with features that are definitively chiseled. Everything about him is *neat*. The double-breasted suit. The understated tie. The polished loafers. But, as warned, this tells you not very much about how the man appears. What is it about physical features, the eyes particularly, that arrange themselves to suggest intelligence, orderliness, and character, even? Certainly it has little, if anything, to do with the size or shape of the features or where they fall on the face. The real differences in what faces tell us are so subtle as to be well beyond the capacity of language to measure.

"We'd like you to do a short interview on film first. Then we should be ready to have lunch and hear your remarks. We are running on time."

I am not surprised. I go into the banquet room, which has

been partitioned to half its full size by a wall that has been moved into place behind a three-foot-high dais. There appear to be about a hundred people in the room. They are all black. Other than that, nothing obvious seems to join them in any common purpose. They range from infant to elderly. While there are more men than women, there are more women than the organization's name gave me to expect. Most of the assembled are in business dress.

Conspicuously, however, at a near left table close to the door (table number twenty-four) are seated four young men in oversized shirts and baggy, low-belted trousers. I cannot read their face maps and feel mildly alienated by their dress. I cannot pinpoint when I first felt a conscious social remove from the young, but, at age fifty-eight, I have felt it towards some (it's the dress I think) for a good time now. I feel it acutely now towards the four young men wearing outsize clothes seated at table twenty-four.

"Mr. Robinson, I am Reverend [I didn't catch his name]."

He is a young preacher, I observe, as if there were something inherently incongruous in his being both young and a preacher. "You and I went to the same high school."

We have not yet been asked by the event organizers to take our seats and thus we are standing amongst milling people near the dais.

"You're from Richmond?" I ask.

"Yes, I run a program for at-risk young black men in Richmond." With mild, unintended discourtesy, my concentration abandons me. I look across the assemblage without knowing that I am trying to find a familiar face. I find none.

". . . do you think that might be possible?"

"I'm sorry, what did you say?"

"Do you think it might be possible to have you come to Richmond sometime to speak to our young men?"

"Yes, of course." I mean the words as I speak them.

We are asked to take our assigned places. I find my name tent on the dais between the lectern and a tent marked with the name *Peewee Kirkland*. I am alone on the dais. I welcome the respite. I fuddle through the printed program to find my place in the order of speakers. The shredded lettuce and tomato wedges herald the institutional fare with which we are shortly to be assaulted. I look out again at the conferees, moving purposefully now to find table numbers that correspond to their tickets. Again, I can identify no talking heads, *experts*, media bees, ambition junkies, spin people, or celebrity liars. The *beautiful people*, overrepresented in Washington, are not here. I surmise that the luncheon is not a fund-raiser to which the organizers have sought to draw people by using celebrities as magnets. From what I can tell, all of the people here work in the regional programs of the host organization.

Another look around the room leaves me with a vague sensation of apartness. I venture no further toward self-understanding, although a rebukeful truism runs unbidden along the edge of my thoughts: *There is no shortage of those who come to do good and stay to do well.*

"Hey, good brother, I'm Peewee." Though not particularly tall, the person sitting next to and speaking to me is a rangy man who moves with the unmistakable mannerism of the athlete. His hair is long in the Afro style of the sixties. His fifty-four-year-old, not unhandsome face bears the mark of street experience. He talks. I listen. I am preoccupied with thoughts of how to gauge my remarks to an audience I do not know. But even with the half mind that listens, I understand little of what he says to me. Several times over lunch he uses the phrase *keep it real*. He is using it as a verb, a noun, a system of philosophy. I have no idea what he means by the phrase in any of its usages: "It's just a keep-it-real thing, you know."

But I do not *know*.

Somewhere over the years, I think, I must have lost track of the language Peewee is speaking. Perhaps I knew it long ago as a boy in another world when all my friends appeared to have only nicknames. *Saddle Head. Smut. Sunky Britches. Freak.* Countless *Boo*s and as many *Bay Bruh*s. But for me now, assuming I'd ever mastered it, the language of that distant past had become a lost art. I could no longer see back around the long arc of my life to the mean space of the early poverty that had formed my emotional politics.

The politics had remained constant enough. But the privation on which the politics had originally been constructed had long since become an academic memory. I am no longer poor. And virtually all of the blacks I have come to know, talk to, work with, and befriend over the past thirty-five years speak and think as I do. Somehow in the subtle desensitizing embrace of life's myriad upward transitions, I fear I may have lost the heart's knowledge of the social slice from whence I sprang, although I am conscious of none of this.

"... I had the move 'foe Pearl had it." Peewee is telling me that he pioneered the reverse dribble. My attention has graduated to full-listen and half-belief.

"I played basketball in college," I tell Peewee. *Trumps.*

"Where?" asks Peewee.

"Norfolk State from '59 to '62."

"I played for Norfolk State myself," says Peewee, "in the sixties."

Yeah, right.

We have finished the entree and begun eating the cold apple pie that, along with the salad, had arrived at our tables before we had. Mark Lawrence, who had been out of the room for upwards of a half hour, is walking towards the dais, presumably to begin the program.

". . . college is giving me an honorary doctorate degree and I'm finishing up my master's now." This from Peewee. I do not believe him.

I have scribbled some talking points on a napkin, but I will not look at them after I begin to speak. Still, I need the scrap of paper.

Mark Lawrence is a polished and well-educated (Wharton Business School, Cornell) man, and he makes the tasteful, well-prepared introduction one would expect of him. Upon my arrival I had asked him what he wanted me to say, thinking he would ask me to stick to the more domestic themes of male mentorship. Surprisingly he had said, "Why don't you talk about what you're writing about now, the case for black reparations." I was surprised by his suggestion because I had not raised the positions I was taking in *The Debt* to any audience, or to *anyone* for that matter other than Hazel, and I had no notion of how my ideas might be received.

America's cultural climate is antihistory, antimemory, thus, it is not easy to draw a line from any contemporary social condition back to genesis events that unfolded hundreds of years ago. Americans generally, black and white, have no memory of anything much more than a pop song ago and assume reflexively that whatever *is*, always *was*, as if a discernible contemporary unequal economic relationship of racial groups was fixed in nature as predictably as the rotation of interplanetary bodies.

But how in America had great wealth and great poverty begun their paths apart? How had the lines of privilege and privation, as mirror opposites, verged over the American centuries away from each other? How had the lines become all too nearly coextensive with race? How had the mortar of memory dried dust hard, sealing with it its own cold explanation, held fast from all. Blanket amnesia favors the thief. This is my thought as I rise to speak.

I look at Peewee and, for the first time, suspect that behind his costume of syntax, he may be north of my estimate. I warn myself that I must not be misled by the hip-hop in his talk. It occurs to me that I, a victim of prejudice, am not without a set of my own.

As for the line that verges inexorably upwards, I had an experience only a few days ago that has, I believe, a place here. I had been visited by a largely black delegation, a member of which was a white scion of old and bottomless wealth. The young man had accomplished nothing of consequence in his own right and was only in the meeting because he bore a last name that signaled money.

I am embarrassed to confess that I accorded the young man (younger than two of my three children) a measure of reflexive respect. This response was particularly insupportable given the *nothing* I knew about the young man and the *something* I did know about his parents, who were, among other things, money pillars of the Democratic Party.

It seems that not long before, the scion's mother had hosted a sleepover for a younger daughter's private-school friends and greeted, the morning after, the mother of the one black invitee thusly: "I understand that your daughter attends our school on financial aid. Is that so?" "Yes," answered the black mother, humiliated. "Well, if she works hard and marries well, she should be all right," said scion mother.

The humiliated black mother's inability to pay the seventeen-thousand-dollar annual tuition had been every bit as inherited as the wealthy white mother's easy wherewithal to do so. But this was completely unperceived and meant no more to the wealthy socialite than any possible explanation of how the financial gap between her and the black mother may have developed over time in the first place.

Lastly on this point, the scion seated in my office, a much admired member of Washington society and rich beyond belief, proved himself upon opening his mouth to be as dumb as a brick.

Click.

I have still not decided upon the structure of my remarks or even how I am to begin. I look at the audience for what seems longer than actual time. I sense already that these are not people for whom oratory without prescription suffices. The problems they face are as new as this morning, as critical as a client's dollar meal, as lethal as fresh insult, old privation, a vial of crack.

They look at me. *Well?*

"To understand our dilemma as a people in the world, our contemporary circumstance of underclassness in America, we must be able to draw a line back through time to the origins of our crisis, from our current relative poverty to the harsh century of legal racial discrimination which preceded it and from there back to the two hundred forty-six years of American slavery, which left us impoverished, illiterate, psychologically damaged, and stripped of any memory of who we had been before slavery in the early centuries of a long and unquestioned era of

African global achievement . . ." My voice is quiet, not by device, but with a graveness compelled by the theme of my introductory comments. There are murmurs of approval. I raise my eyes to meet theirs, and in them I see my own. We are all victims. This, in the absence of memory, is what binds us.

Could there be one here whose forebear was sold by Jefferson to restock his wine cellar? Is not this color-motley array evidence enough of the systematic rape of our grandmothers? Might not the empty chair at table four well enough symbolize the lost bloodlines of long-dead black grandfathers whose penises were cut off by white South Carolina slave owners whose descendants in Columbia wrap themselves even now in the bloody flag of their beastly heritage?

The Catholics of Northern Ireland have given their problem (like ours, centuries in duration) a name. They call it *the troubles*. We have not done so. They know the antecedent events of their dilemma whereas we've been deprived of learning ours. We only know keenly the damnable condition we are in. Little of how or whence or from whom it developed. Families had been torn asunder—husband from wife, mother, father from child—and lost with them, the priceless fabric of timeless cultures. Tantamount was it to the modern interrogation of torture victims, stripped of their self-esteem, a thousand victims keening alone in a thousand lightless, airless chambers. Seeing things, hearing voices, remembering little. Forever.

Black events, no matter the occasion, invariably bear the mark of the unnamed *problem*. It is there as we laugh. It is there as we mourn. It is here now. Einstein had proposed that distance and time are not absolute, that intervals of time are affected by the motion of those who observe time's elapse. So much has befallen us for so long that we feel powerless on the limitless landscape of time, except to perceive it in distortion, as if the future had already happened and we were awaiting its verdict.

My eyes come to rest on the occupants of table number twenty-four. I cannot read their feelings. I pay particular attention to one at the table I had noticed coming into the room. His right forearm bears a tattoo of elaborate lettering spelling out in caps the word *RACE*. The word and its position on the young man's arm summon for me now a meaning different no doubt than that which the young man himself had intended.

South Carolina's slave-plantation owners had known nothing about how to grow and irrigate rice. That knowledge was brought to the low country by Africans stolen from Sierra Leone by the Royal African Company of England. As the slaves produced the rice that made the plantation owners rich, their glistening backs bore the branded acronym of their corporate captors: *R.A.C.E.*

"... and as a result of all that we have been caused to endure—from slavery to the new legal racial bondage of the twentieth century—an economic gap continues to separate blacks and whites in America. This gap is static and structural. For two hundred and forty-six years *our* uncompensated labor launched wealthy institutions and private corporate fortunes in America such as Brown University and Fleet Bank, both founded by the Brown brothers, who got their start in American business building slave ships and investing in the slave trade. Cotton made everyone associated with it wealthy—the plantation owners, the brokers, the shippers, the shipbuilders, the jobbers, the United States treasury—everyone became rich except the people who produced the cotton.

"They—we—us—our forebears—were stripped of everything—the value of our labor, our mothers, our fathers, our children, and by the tens of millions, our very lives. And so my friends, let us tell our young that we are behind in America not because there is anything wrong with *us*, but rather, that something heinous happened a long time ago and continued for a long time after. Tell them that our people have a proud and ancient history that must be told to them, that slavery robbed us of warranted wealth and memory, that slavery extended under new guises well into the twentieth century, that we have endured in America every imaginable discrimination for three hundred and forty-six years. Tell them we have been the victims of the longest-running crime against humanity in the world over the last five hundred years. And lastly, tell them that like all other peoples in the world who've suffered human rights crimes at the hands of governments—Jews, Koreans, Japanese-Americans—we too must be compensated by the government complicit in the crime against us, the United Sates of America."

I sit down. They stand up. Do not misunderstand this report of their spirited approval as a boast of any sort. The speech was neither particularly eloquent nor insightful. I had simply spoken my heart, a heart born of the same hard experience as theirs. Only the voice—a medium, no more—had been mine. All the rest—the thoughts, the sentiments, the visceral knowings—moved around and through us all like the plaintive ghosts of forebears awaiting remembrance and redress.

Mark Lawrence now prepares to present a public service award. I do not catch the name of the award. Somewhere in a subconscious storeroom for the unimportant, I've long since arrived at a belief that awards are given out of some curious planner's need to protract luncheon programs, a need that runs illogically crosswise to the unspoken desire of all guests everywhere to have their speakers brief, their award recipients, if forced upon them, silent, and their hard-bun captivity mercifully ended. No program-ending benediction anywhere was ever met with displeasure.

Mr. Lawrence has on the lectern before him two or three typed pages, presumably descriptive of the award and the honoree. He does not read from the pages. Instead, with unusual conviction, he extemporizes: "I have known this man for several years now, and no one more perfectly exemplifies the values of our programs than he does. He is the heart and soul of our efforts to pull our young men back from the brink." Mr. Lawrence continues in this vein for a time before announcing, "Our 1999 public service award goes to . . ."

My attention had wavered. I look out over the audience for someone to stand and begin moving towards the dais. Amidst applause, Peewee pulls his chair back, inadvertently bumping mine, stands, and moves behind me towards Mr. Lawrence, who awaits him with a broad smile and outstretched arms. I do my best to mask surprise. Mr. Lawrence hands a brass-and-wood plaque to Peewee. The applause continues.

Before it subsides and Peewee has a chance to say anything, the occupants of table twenty-four rise and stride in a rolling gait towards the dais. The apparent leader is tall and wiry with a wispy mustache and chin hair. I estimate that he is in his early twenties, although he seems somehow older, as if the boy in the man had departed prematurely. He does not smile, which deepens the impression.

The other three are even taller than their wiry leader, now two feet from the steps at the end of the dais. As the leader steps onto the end of the dais, the particleboard of the dais step creaks under the weight of the second man, who must weigh well over 240 pounds. The board creaks a second and then a third time. They are all big men. My chair feet lose purchase on the boards of the dais as the four young men rumble across the shallow platform toward Peewee Kirkland, Mr. Lawrence, and me.

The apartness again. When had it begun? This only just recognizable feeling of estrangement? As a badge of sorts, I claim as foundation for all my serious exertions a bond with Africa's issue whom I need so much to measure ennobled by resilience to victimization and hardship. Had Marley's early death been a kindness after all? Had his anthem plea been naïve? *Keep your culture. Rasta man stand up. Congo man don't give up.* Had our way back to self-knowledge been finally and irretrievably lost?

I look again at the four men moving towards me. Images are conjured of names in the papers: Tupac Shakur, Biggie Smalls, Eazy-E. All of a new and fatalist class, trapped on a treadmill running wildly out of control. All living fast under a lightless, near inescapable pall of death. All expecting death, forecasting it. All finding it, and finding it violently.

Peewee says into the microphone, "These are my guys," and the wiry leader moves to the lectern with a loop-cool fluidness that is different in its motion from my generation's. Ours was a similarly lyrical motion, but with a dip in it that would cause us to lose and gain up to four inches in height with each stride. The current young black man's walk has more sway in it. There is still dip in the step, but it is less pronounced and more toward the horizontal. The walk is smoother than ours, with the shoulders describing slow figure eights inside baggy tops. I don't recall that the black women of my generation had a discernible walk. (This would indicate that they were more secure than we.

A startling insight.) This was, however, decades before *the neck*, a mannerism about which nothing salubrious can be said.

Of course, Marley was too late and he knew it. We could not *keep* our culture. We could only try to reassemble that which had been brutally and systematically stripped from us during slavery, leaving us vulnerable and lost in the world, within and without Africa.

> *I ask myself who I am. I wear another's clothes. I speak another's language. I worship another's god. I practice another's customs. I recite another's history. I ask myself who I am and I can not answer. Instead, I invent myself, every lifetime, sometimes every day. Sometimes the walk is all that I have to call my own.*

"My name is New Child and I want to say a few words about my man Peewee." He speaks in a slightly hoarse voice. He smiles and looks much younger than at first sighting. "You know, Peewee, man, he saved my life. Me and the guys here be dead if it wasn't for Peewee."

I look at Peewee and begin to feel what? Well, uh, less judgmental.

"When everybody had gave up on me, you know, my teachers, my dad I don't even really remember. When I was 'bout to git killed, Peewee was the only one that cared. He talked and talked and talked to me. He knew. He been there. He saved me. He saved all of us." New Child looks at one of his boys whose name is Furious Stylze. Furious nods assent.

The day before, I had spent hours slogging through volumes of World Trade Organization material written in maze-speak about intellectual property rights and implications for global trade. You see, my principal career "address" for the last twenty-five years has been in the rarefied world of clinical public policy, a world in which shiny "street signs" bear aseptic names like *U.S. interests*, *free trade*, *privatization*, and *export-import*. The "streets" are found in expensive "neighborhoods" on which billions of taxpayer dollars have been lavished.

Take for instance the ill-starred, but ritzy, Washington "suburb" once called Super-Conducting Super-Collider. A poll had revealed that no one in the entire metropolitan area of Cleveland had ever even heard of Super-Conducting Super-Collider, or "SC Twice" as the pork-barrel enclave became known to the members of the U.S. Senate Appropriations Committee.

Owing to this, at least in part, the Congress had ladled out $13 billion of our hard-earned dollars to the enclave with no return at all. The money had been just shot all to hell. Much the same could be said of other gilded sinkhole Capitol Hill neighborhoods such as Star Wars and F-16 and Stealth Bomber (found to be unusable in rain).

I sit here on the dais having landed in a new world, a world foreign to me, and more foreign still to the gilded sinkholes. I am embarrassed by this realization, not least because this *new* world is anything but new, and a branch of it is physically situated only blocks from where I live and is just as near to Gilded Sinkhole Central, the U.S. Capitol.

". . . we didn't have nothing and no matter how hard we worked, we wasn't gonna never have nothing."

I am paying close attention to New Child now. He is surprisingly confident and self-possessed. He continues to speak, and the exterior of him that I had first thought menacing now seems to belie interior qualities that show him in a much different light.

"My mom did the best she could for us. She worked hard

for nothing. The schools wasn't no good. I wanted what everybody else in this country wanted, but the system didn't give us no chance to get what a lot of people in this country have. No chance." He pauses and looks meditative. He has lived all of his life in Harlem and knows only a few in this audience. I wonder if this has made him circumspect. He glances at his boys.

"And so when I was twelve years old, I started in the life of crime. I met Peewee when I was sixteen. If I hadn't met Peewee, I be dead now. We all be dead."

I benefit from an accident of birth, which is all that distinguishes my lot from New Child's. I have lived longer and viewed a much different existential scenery, either directly from comfortable vantage points or indirectly through formal education. My information is thousands of years old. It carries forward over time's mountains and hills and valleys. New Child's life is short. He has had little formal education. Valley is all that he knows. It's long shadows bound the beginning and end of all the world he has ever seen. Valley, for him, is a hard anchorage, a birth and life sentence, an unrefusable bequest with all of its material and cultural implications.

I listen to him now in light of a Black Entertainment Television special I had recently seen. The show had marked the twentieth anniversary of the network, making it nearly as old as New Child. In twenty years, the show's youthful host had said, Black Entertainment Television had established itself as the fount of black music culture. Twenty years against the ages. How damnably depressing it was. Twenty years of coarse moment, a moment that, alas, coincides with the arrival of the information age, a moment that covers nearly the whole of New Child's life, blurring the moment's aberrance.

Tens of millions of New Childs, valley-stuck, blind beyond

their culture's near and far ranges, shown *this* for their people's whole artistic output. *Fount crudely claimed.* Male performers yanking their crotches. Nubile women dancers, their sex straining against flexing thongs, shimmying their behinds before cameras that beam the behinds as heralds of *black culture* with electronic-age efficiency to the far corners of the universe. Somewhere along the way, the host had introduced a male singer as *the* artist to whose rhythmic stylings blacks make babies. *Hootchie cootchie rom. Cable surround. Syncopated plague.*

A mere forty years ago television pictures had helped create the civil rights movement. The pictures, more than anything else, conveyed to the nation the nobility and eloquence of anonymous bravery. They captured on film the quality of courage that delivered otherwise ordinary people from servile compliance to noble defiance. Not just leaders, but simple blacks from all walks, risked their lives pulling themselves erect in the hate-filled cauldrons of the Deep South to face down guns and dogs and hoses and steepled hoods on night-riding sheets.

Television cameras documented all, transmitting grainy black-and-white images of selfless heroism to rapt viewers around the world, rejuvenating old social justice movements and precipitating new ones, unnerving despots and innervating their downtrodden prey.

When had African-Americans been depicted in a better light? And not just those directly visible in it, singing their freedom songs and taking the blows, but those long gone who might have believed in a last earthly thought their mortal sacrifices to have been made in vain. From some ethereal realm, might possibly Gabriel Prosser, Harriet Tubman, and Denmark Vesey have been able to read on the visage of Selma's dauntless children the emboldening marks of the forebears' first strikes against slavery? Might DuBois have at last rested redeemed?

In my lifetime, the civil rights movement of the 1950s and 1960s had been our finest hour. I had been a college student. I was in it. The world saw it on television. It saw black bodies hanging by the neck behind the firelit grin-grimace of whites. It saw neatly dressed young black men and women sitting in at lunch counters under racial epithets, hostile looks, and saliva rain. It saw four small black girl-child bodies removed from the rubble of a Birmingham church. It saw an unbudgeable people.

The world saw it all—on global television.

One of the movement's important leaders was the Reverend Walter Fauntroy, a disciple of Dr. Martin Luther King Jr.'s. Years later, the Reverend Fauntroy would become a member of the U.S. Congress representing the District of Columbia. He would continue to fight for the fundamental rights of the poor. He would be arrested alongside me in an effort to end apartheid in South Africa. He would lead a life of social service. He would never become rich.

The beneficiaries of the civil rights movement number globally in the hundreds of millions. I am one such beneficiary. Another is Robert Johnson. Decades ago, Congressman Walter Fauntroy gave Mr. Johnson a job. The civil rights movement gave him a chance.

Gossamer-clad buttocks shimmy closer to the lens of camera one. The imagination is not taxed. Camera two pans an audience of black female faces framed by bone-straight blond wigs. The camera moves, stops, and focuses on Robert Johnson, the founder and CEO of Black Entertainment Television, America's only black-owned television network. Across the world, more people will see the BET twentieth-anniversary special than saw Rosa Parks forty-five years thence sitting alone on a Montgomery bus.

New Child is young. He has never seen Rosa Parks. He *has* seen Mr. Johnson and much of his programming.

Syncopated plague.

"We heard what you was saying, Mr. Robinson."

I am stirred from my reverie. New Child continues his remarks while looking at me. "We gon git the reparations. My generation gon git what we owed."

I don't know him. I don't know what he knows. But his persona is, both, encouraging and discouraging. He has an apparent abundance of spirit and confidence, but obvious disabilities as well that are born of socialization and are virtually irreversible. He does not speak majority-culture-success English. I reflect again on his speech and mannerisms. I conclude that these characteristics give rise to a certain prejudice to which even I am not immune and, in any case, for the sake of fairness, must be put in context.

New Child is a flesh-and-blood distillation of American social statistics that would embarrass any number of less shameless nations. You will forgive me if I sound a little preachy. I detest preachiness and promise to fight its temptation for the balance of this telling. But the American social experience contorts all black development, mine included.

Often it would appear that blacks are constrained to select from a four-item life-chance wine list of varietal American poisons:

> The Walk *The Walk, sometimes called dregs brew, is the oldest American red wine, produced in Jamestown, Vir-*

ginia, since 1619 exclusively for blacks systematically denied any and everything else: social, economic, and educational opportunity. The substance, which is administered involuntarily to poor blacks, produces in its prospectless consumers the lone career outcome allowed to them, an artistic but exaggerated walk unseen anywhere in the middle and upper reaches of American society, black or white.

The Talk *The Talk is a full-throated zinfandel produced in America since the mid-twentieth-century for blacks who speak majority-culture-success English and advocate the full economic and political empowerment of all blacks. Owing to certain structural racial and class impediments inherent in the general society, the wine produces but one allowed result: a desired (by its producers) preachiness or steam-venting from its relatively more comfortable but powerless consumers who are in no other way much different from the consumers of the Walk.*

The Take *The Take is a paper-dry, expensive white wine enjoyed by a very small number of whites as well as blacks.*

Take users (or takers) are usually rich or single-mindedly on their way towards becoming rich. Consumer surveys have revealed that takers prefer the wine not only for its magical lightness but also for its career-assisting property of sharpening innate greed and loosening natural inhibitions associated with moral memory and conscience. The bottle label suggests that the wine be served colder than those aforementioned and that the wine's avarice-related properties are best realized when the taker drinks alone. The label also suggests something about the presence or absence of mirrors, but I cannot remember which it is. Lastly, the label informs that the top one percent of Americans control as much wealth as the bottom ninety-five percent. This does not appear to lessen the admiration of the nontakers for the takers.

The Headache

The Headache is a fruity, amber-colored, crossover wine used by well-educated, well-intentioned, dedicated, professional blacks who, from a variety of nominally important posts, work with and within local and national white power structures to defend as

*best they can the interests of the black
community. Consumers of this wine
are known to have Headaches daily.*

The marbles of such seriocomic thoughts roll around in my head as I listen to New Child. This is flight and I know it. I daydreamed as a child in school. I do it still as an adult.

New Child's youthful energy of hope damns the false confidence with which I earlier spoke. But why has my confidence waned? Could it be that I know too much, that I have seen too much? Doubtful. From what I can guess, for all my years, I have seen mercifully less than he has in his few. But this is certainly a mistake, if not of logic, of language at least. New Child has *suffered*, yes. But how much can he have *seen*? Likely, precious little, precisely owing to all that he has suffered. We are all (black, white, brown) world-flung, mindless yields of social inheritance. Why do we talk as we talk? Assume as we assume? Expect as we expect? Hope as we hope? The answers hide from us in the secrets of back-filed memory. They skulk in the shadows of forgotten history, obscured by tenacious privilege resting oblivious and merry atop plinths of privation and self-doubt.

Katrina Brown, a white de Wolf family descendent of the de Wolf slave-owning family, writes:

*What do we inherit from seven generations ago? From five?
What do we inherit from our grandparents, a face, a laugh, a
ring, a Bible, table manners, a name? What do we inherit without realizing it? What family secrets hide in the unspoken and
unseen? New England where my mother's family is from has its
share of unacknowledged ghosts. My cousins call it the deep north.*

33

At twenty-nine when I was finally ready to look at our family's history, I discovered that I was descended from the largest slave-trading family in early America. From 1789 to 1820, fathers, sons, and grandsons in the de Wolf family of Bristol, Rhode Island, developed a triangle (slave) trade. . . .

Poor onion farmers turned slave traders—fathers, sons, cousins, uncles, and in-laws were captains and sailors, auctioneers, plantation owners and overseers, insurers and bankers and lawyers of the family trade. . . .

One of the de Wolfs, James, at the end of his life in 1837 was the second richest man in the United States. He served in the United States Senate and secured a political favor from President Thomas Jefferson that enabled the de Wolfs to continue in the slave trade long after it had become illegal. . . . After the slave trade, [the de Wolfs] became ministers and bishops, writers and professors, artists and architects, upright Yankees with our faces to the wind.

Tens of thousands of men, women, and children who looked like New Child suffered under the lash on de Wolf plantations, distilleries, and ships that plied the high seas from Rhode Island to West Africa, and from there to Cuba and Georgia.

How many such stories are there? How many surviving American private fortunes were constructed upon the wearied backs of slaves? How many businesses? How many Aetnas and Fleet Banks can be called to account for tarnished histories? How many respected universities, the Browns, the Georgetowns, owe their beginnings to the bestial abuse of slavery? Hundreds? Thousands? More? How many *Hartford Courant*s ran ads to facilitate the apprehension of runaway slaves? How vast was (is) the network? At how many intersections did the benefit currents cross? How complex remains the latticework? How witting are the intergenerational beneficiaries in their ride aboard the victims, then and now? How many innocent Christian white people have there been to live well on the blind lovely side of hate, thriving in a white society's civil interstices as guiltless as white clapboard on a leafy lane? How many know? How many care?

New Child is alive, and that is something.

". . . I put God in my life and God is on our side," says New Child to applause. I am moved by what he says but . . . "God"? Do not the disciples of privilege invoke the same God and declare for Him a preference for faux-Tudor architecture? Do they not see Him sitting amongst them in endowed pews of the Sabbath's vain mansions? Do they not publish their trust in Him on the coin of the realm? Do they not thank Him? For grandfather's bequest? For Aunt Gertrude's Waterford? For the volume control to vox populi? For civil peace? For advantage, the charlatan's imprecation? For prosperity and compounding abundance? For the hallucinogen of manifest destiny? For forgiveness? Would a God that performs such for *them* do anything for New Child?

Edward Ball, descendent of one of South Carolina's largest slave-holding families, writes:

> *In childhood, I remember feeling an intangible sense of worth that might be linked to the old days. Part of the feeling came from the normal encouragements of parents who wanted their children to rise. An equal part came from an awareness that long ago our family had lived like lords and that the world could still be divided into the pedigreed and the rootless.*
>
> *The invitation to the family reunion sat on my desk, beckoning.*

No one among the Balls talked about how slavery had helped us, but whether we acknowledged it or not, the powers of our ancestors were still in hand. Although our social franchise had shrunk, it had nevertheless survived. If we did not inherit money, or land, we received a great fund of cultural capital, including prestige, a chance at education, self-esteem, a sense of place, mobility, even (in some cases) a flair for giving orders. And it was not only "us," the families of former slave-owners, who carried the baggage of the plantations. By skewing things so violently in the past, we had made sure that our cultural riches would benefit all white Americans.

"We be dead man if it wasn't for Peewee. He was there for me when nobody else was." Peewee stands and embraces New Child, and then Furious Stylze, a friend of New Child's.

Something significant is occurring in the room. To me at least. I cannot name the feeling but it is similar to the mildly disturbing vertigo one feels when looking at a big object (like a large painting) placed too close to the eye. Before, I was certain. Now, I am not. Of what? I have no crystallized idea. But it must have something to do with my lifelong fascination (obsession even) with things, issues, people, places that are distant.

I live in the District of Columbia but I don't know how to locate the voting wards on a city map. I know more about Bujumbura, Burundi. Why is this? I am always interested in *there*.

For the same reason, I am forced to concede, that the nitwit prizes the senator over the schoolteacher, the entrepreneur over the social worker. Arrogance is armored stupidity. But even arrogance is easiest to spot from a distance. I am being as clear on this point as the limits on self-exposure will permit.

Rationalizing, I could reason, painful though it would be,

that I am no different from anyone else, that I, like tens of millions of other wanderlust victims, am an easy mark for the Somewhere Else industry. Once in an airport in Paris, as flights where chimed and announced to all corners of the globe, I could not distinguish the frenetic and pointless scurry of the ants at my feet from the galloping hordes of overstressed tourists who seemed willing to mash anything underfoot, ants and small children included, so long as it put them on their way to somewhere else. Places and faces fascinate us for no other reason than millions have heard of them and they are not next door. This phenomenon is not classified as a form of mental illness for no other reason than most humans appear to suffer from it.

I go to such introspective lengths here because those who describe themselves as leaders in our community would do well to undertake similar self-examination. I have known well by now enough "leaders" to know that what passes as leadership is often little more than an expression of egoism. It would appear that a condition of such leadership in the black community is the accomplishment of a relative celebrity that varies directly with the rung-level assignment of the leader's status in the broader American community. To Americans, black and white, Jesse Jackson Sr. is a black "leader." James Comer, the brilliant black professor of child psychiatry at the Yale University Child Study Center, is not a "leader," although he is a seminal and influential American thinker on early childhood education for disadvantaged children. His writings are deeply influencing what Americans know about how children learn. Peewee Kirkland, on the strength of firsthand witness, saves lives. Nonetheless, Peewee is not a "leader."

Dr. Comer and Peewee are not "leaders" because they are not famous in relative terms. They are doing different forms of public service with broad and constructive implications for the future of the black community and America in general. They are leaders who, to become "leaders," would have to actively pursue fame or be captured fortuitously in the coinciding frames of serious work and the frippery light of public notice. Such unassisted coincidences occur about as frequently as a solar eclipse.

Leaders and "leaders" move in all but mutually exclusive constellations. More often than not the former pursue concrete objectives, the latter attention. In rare instances, because of high public interest (pro and con) in the social objectives sought, public notice attaches to authentic leaders. Martin Luther King, Malcolm X, and Ralph Nader are modern examples of this.

In general and with particular application for the black community, American society has at present saddled itself with an unconstructive and contorted definition of what a leader is or should strive to be. This has rather muddled all of our thinking, and as you may discern from the foregoing, mine included.

Peewee is receiving a standing ovation. They all know who he is. He stands at the lectern for a long while waiting for the room to settle. New Child, Furious, and the two others, whose names I did not catch, return to table twenty-four.

2

MY THOUGHTS AS
PEEWEE WAITS
TO SPEAK

I look at the young people in the room. *They cannot know how badly my generation has failed them.*

To the innocent victims, it may have seemed as if some inert and ageless sentinel-force were keeping them vertically gaped wide down from the mainstream all this time. The rope somehow slipping eternally well greased.

Despite the catchy fulminations of a president elected by their parents, poor children were poorer under Clinton than they had been twenty years before in the age of Reagan. Their raw numbers had expanded as well. When they were equipped to think the puzzle through, the children still had to have been mystified. You see, their predicament was a most debated American political subject. Pundits pontificated. Politicians stumped. Grantors disbursed. Legislators legislated. Monographists polysyllabified. (Polygraphists might have served the public interest better here.) Academics wrote unread books on the public stipend. Education bureaucrats at all levels replicated themselves like algae in a warm swamp.

The Battle of the Bromides was ever joined. The Republicans: *Do nothing.* The Democrats: *Do something.* The experts:

Do this or (when the child has a spool-shaped cerebellum) *that.* The bureaucrats: *Do funding.* The preachers: *Do Lawd.* (One young, white Chicago priest, Martin Boyd, who worked hard to serve the poor black youth of his parish, had been with some asperity referred to by his fellows of the cloth as St. Martin-in-the-Fields).

At the Odors of Dying Rome Bistro across the street from the Department of Human Services, well-dressed and newly arrived public servants lobbied an imperious maître d' for placement at tables relinquished by public servants departing official Washington with the outgoing administration. Through zippy repartee about numeral-named federal programs for the poor, tuxedoed waiters swirled under silver platters laden with continental fare. A civilized din. The tinkle of cutlery. 'Twas the music of upper-midlevel privilege. Just above the concert could be heard the phrase "midnight basketball" followed by a spray of unkind laughter.

Only days before, in Philadelphia, a reform-minded school superintendent, frustrated by the undertow of the city's politics, had heroically resigned his position. I had been in town at the time to address three hundred African-American, Latino, and Asian high school students who were enrolled in a summer program called Freedom School.

The meeting was held in a hot, poorly lit, narrow, below-ground room in an antediluvian step-down structure just across a busy street from the inner-city campus of Temple University. Two months before, the program's organizers had written me that the students were reading *The Debt*: "Would you come and discuss it with them? These are good young people who have been disillusioned during the regular school term but have worked very hard on all their assignments in Freedom School.

They have been reading your book and preparing lists of questions to ask you. Will you come?"

"Yes, I will," I wrote back immediately. Riding in from Thirtieth Street Station, I was told that the school superintendent, the protector of the Freedom School's funding, had quit.

It never ceases to amaze me how effective whoever the cog-turners are that operate these things can be in arranging the knowledge gaps that separate young from old, unpoor from poor, white from practically everybody else.

"Mr. Robinson, what exactly were you getting at when you wrote on page 147 that . . ." And so it went.

They had zealously prepared. Poor inner-city teenagers, mostly black with uneven regular-school attendance records, showing up on time every morning to a creditless summer-school hot box of academic rigor. They were studying Africa, Latin America, Asia, the world, and life itself. They were discovering themselves. They were glimpsing possibility. They were rapping and dancing and cheering each other on. They were fearing as well that the cheerless "system" would sit on them again soon as it had reliably all of their short lives.

"In September, they return to the teachers who do not respect them," a black teacher had said to me. "Next summer this program may not exist."

I looked at him. He, more than any program of labyrinthine, cross-referenced eligibility criteria, guidelines, and conditions, was the reason for the young people's learning enthusiasm. But he and his staff would be canceled along with the program.

It would seem odd indeed, were it not intended, that the only government programs to work efficiently would be those designed to further enrich the rich: tax shelters, loan guarantees, price supports, and defense contracts, to name a few. Or to go on for a length or two: bankruptcy reform, the death of a patients' rights bill, the minuscule royalties paid by oil companies for use of public lands, the defeat of higher pollution standards by the auto industry, the ethanol subsidy, the sugar subsidy, communications deregulation, utilities deregulation, bank deregulation, a congress that allows corporate tax write-offs for grossly high executive salaries and blocks a one-dollar increase in the minimum wage.

"The superintendent worked hard to change this place," the black teacher told me. "The test scores moved up a little, but these big systems are very hard to change."

The idealistic teacher armed with his Ph.D. was little more than thirty and yet to tire. But the river against whose course he worked flows ceaselessly northward.

In 1960, the top 20 percent of the world's population held 70 percent of the world's wealth, the bottom 20 percent, 2.3 percent. By the year 2000, the top 20 percent had gotten control of 86 percent of the world's wealth while the bottom 20 percent clung to less than 1 percent. Towards the end of the greatest growth surge in global economic history, 2.5 billion people would have to survive on less than two dollars a day. The programs for the top 20 percent—NAFTA, IMF, WTO, OPIC—had worked efficiently enough. Little had worked for the poor.

The exclusive north escalator's ugly, greasy, grinding guts were covered by gleaming pewter-colored treads. Little sound could be heard. A mild whirring beneath a civilized din. A tinkle of cutlery. The scratch of a pen.

Perhaps out of the embarrassment of ostentation, or maybe, more practically, to simply divert attention, the poor, young black American victims were invited to hyena at coarse BET comics and watch a woman's genitalia laid hard against a rope.

The charters of massive American social service agencies are not unlike speed limits. They are written with high intent, posted with methodical care, and observed largely in the breach. Charters are words. Words are not witnesses. Words govern no behavior. Privilege more nearly does. By definition, well-placed privilege trenches under democratic values, offends aspirations of social equality, and bends the public's hires to gray feigning, leaving in its wake for bureaucracy a fouled entablature of American public purpose.

Over the arc of time, the good teacher and the principled bureaucrat arrive to the same forlorn spot, their social commitment transfigured to benign fraud by the impossibility of continued hope and the middle-aged's drug of preference, self-interest. In his short story collection *Lives of the Poets*, E. L. Doctorow saw this dismal truth well: "I have followed it in fidelity, step by step, I have tracked it in its logic, I have never wavered, I have been steadfast, and it has led me to this desert, this flat horizon. I turn around and around and I'm alone. Is there a specific doom that comes of commitment?"

On the train home that night from Philadelphia, I read in the *Washington Post* that 83 schools in the District of Columbia had "met at least four of six goals for improving scores on the standardized test. That compares with 32 schools, of a total of 145, that met similar goals last year."

Only weeks before the results of her stewardship had been announced, Arlene Ackerman, the school superintendent, had been forced to resign. Her mistake: doing her job. In 1996, the District of Columbia Control Board, which for a while ran virtually everything in the city, found that "the test scores of D.C.

public school students in the economically disadvantaged sections of the District have declined at a greater rate than test scores in the more affluent sections of the city, reflecting a disparity in educational outcomes which needs to be remedied by improving educational opportunities in all areas of the District."

To remedy the problem, Ackerman altered the funding formula for the school system in a way that would more equitably meet the needs of *all* seventy thousand of Washington's public school students and not just those who were predominately white, better off, and living west of Rock Creek Park.

Ackerman, who is black, may or may not have known, going in, that those who are white, better off, and living west of Rock Creek Park have at their disposal more time, money, and influence (even in a black-run city) to see after the very *un*commonweal of their kith than do the members of the larger, poorer black community to see after theirs.

The west-of-the-parkers, despite the broad success of the new and more equitable funding formula, did not like the formula and used all of their advantages to run Ackerman out of town. Before her fait became accompli, I'm embarrassed to confess, I knew almost nothing of the unfolding drama. Only as Marc Fisher, a *Washington Post* columnist, hammered the last nail into Ackerman's coffin and the disadvantaged children's prospects did I realize it had long since been *decided* that she must go. Decided? Well, people who are bred to have things their way don't need to assemble in a smoke-filled room.

After Ackerman announced her resignation, the general public learned from the *Post* just how much progress the overall public school population had made during her tenure.

One's thoughts run across wide spaces on a train at night:
How must it feel to be white and privileged? Does one even see

the others? In their apartments, their churches, their workplaces? Does one credit their hopes, assay their humanity, estimate their anger? Is it the effulgence of self-approval that blinds them from seeing out and others from seeing in? Does one know and not care, or can one arrange the conscience like furniture? Or, as the sign promises: Will build to suit . . .

Do they believe their own bullshit? I don't believe mine. Nobody believes their own bullshit, do they? I mean, God, all the crappola about their precious freedoms. It's enough to embarrass a rock.

Can it be argued with a straight face in America that we have a free press? Would I have any less influence over the press were it government-owned? Would it, indeed could it, represent my interest less? The Washington Post *is run by Donald Graham. It is his personal stationery to do with and write on as he pleases. What possibly could his prerogatives and privileges have to do with my freedom?*

AIDS is devastating Africa. I see that in there. Guy writes a book. What's his name? Hooper. Edward Hooper. The River I think the title is. Argues persuasively that AIDS resulted from a mistake made by Western researchers using Congolese as guinea pigs while looking in the fifties for a polio vaccine. Didn't see that in the Post.

Now the U.S. wants to lend African countries money to buy AIDS medicine from U.S. pharmaceutical companies at market prices. Lend. At commercial rates. To buy from huge U.S. drug companies at market price. Didn't see that in there. How goddamn crass. How counterfeit their minuet. How greedy their asses.

How wonderful those kids were tonight. Bet I never see that in anybody's newspaper. Son of a bitch.

Combined in the otherwise empty quiver of Czar Nicholas II were power, wealth, and stunning ordinariness. More weak, witless, and oblivious than mean, Czar Nicholas, before getting his family shot in 1918, managed to plunge "Mother Russia" into famine, war, and ultimately, Bolshevism. While the suffering masses of czarist Russia turned on each other from time to time with criminal expression, the ill-fated, myopic czar saw no reason why the Romanovs would not call their palaces home forever. If the tradition of czarist rule has been long, he might have reasoned, so also must be the future of czarist rule. But the last czar hadn't been a reflective enough man to recognize that in historical terms the life span of moral ostriches is relatively short.

Unhandsome society, which bears aloft the showy edifice of state, invariably rots quietly from the root up, a cell at a time. Unless stood back from at a distance of considerable time, the rot moves unnoticed beneath the ground. Then there is the past's natural penchant to disguise its meaning.

In August 2000, the Russian Orthodox Church formally declared Czar Nicholas II a martyr and a saint for dying at the hands of a Bolshevik firing squad that represented forces that were enemies of the Church.

Time, perhaps the only effective ointment for the lineal scars of great crimes, hides, heals, and confuses all at once.

In America, hope is raised by the ideal of its glorious letter and crushed all at once by the letter's cynical disregard. America is splendid theater for the preservation of those armed with the power to preserve. All else is illusion. Even the well-trumpeted but uncommon successes of the black poor give the illusion its credibility.

If only for a moment I could look backwards from the future. From a vantage point well beyond the time left to me. When America is formed of a new and darker majority. When the unseen are at last centered on the masthead. When little is as it was before. How will such change have been wrought? Through violent upheaval? A visionary's transport of us to higher ground? The slow, steady descent of the self-deceived? Will historians remember the warning candles so little heeded now?

Will they write that America was never an authentic democracy or, worse still, never really tried to be? Will they opine in dreary retrospectives that today's decision-makers erred in ignoring the world's (and its own) lengthening poverty, that, as a practical matter, the error was compounded by the deepening of poverty's appearance under the color of those who had formed America's new majority? Will they notice the role of what will by then smack to them of an avaricious corporatism? Will Ralph Nader, who labored in vain to turn America's overall public policy course, be remembered as John Paul Jones, John Brown, or John Doe?

Will they wonder how the old America had ever seriously called itself a free society in light of an Institute for Policy Studies question: "Does the fact that the United States has less than one-twentieth of the world's population and one-quarter of the world's prisoners suggest there is something fundamentally wrong with our criminal justice system? (Of our 2 million prisoners, 1.2 million of them are behind bars for nonviolent offenses, and poor people—particularly people of color—are disproportionately represented in arrests, conviction, imprisonment, and executions.)"

3

PEEWEE'S SPEECH

The room is quiet. Peewee looks toward his wife, Kleopatra, who sits with their six-year-old son, little Peewee, at a second-row table to his father's right. Peewee Sr.'s eyes move to the left and come to rest on table twenty-four.

"Mark, first let me thank you for this award. It means a lot to me. It also means a lot to my guys here and all the young people we are working to save at the School of Skillz. But before I go any further, I want to thank Kleopatra, who is sitting right here with little Peewee." Peewee Sr. pauses, considering. "What I always wanted to see in a woman had nothing to do with how beautiful she was, or even just, how decent she was. I wanted to see God in a woman. I wanted to be involved with a woman who was extremely godly, but not because she went to church every Sunday, but because she was like that more by nature."

He and Kleopatra look at each other. Their eyes appear to shine. He continues to look at her as he starts again. "When I met Kleopatra . . . I remember the first time I saw her, because we had met on the phone, and she was in New York. I was in Las Vegas. A friend had introduced us on the phone, and I had sent her a scarf after talking to her a couple of times and invited her to Vegas. And when she came, she had to wear the scarf, because I didn't know who she was. And I remember watching her, and just watching the gracefulness in the way she walked. And I was thinking to myself, wow, man, I could see God all through this lady, you know what I mean? And three days later we was married."

I listen to him as he reveals himself enough to gently surprise again a prejudiced expectation.

"When I was a little boy in Spanish Harlem, we was very poor. Our building was bad and dark and dangerous. And all the guys I saw on the streets was involved in the life of crime. I'd hear my mother and father talking about the rent increase and other times about just Christmas and holidays and what they couldn't do, the things they wanted to do and couldn't do. So that created a lot of frustration. Sometimes my father would be laid off, which created another sense of frustration. I remember as the years started going by, and I remember one time just walking in the streets. I was eleven years old, and I walked in the streets just crying to myself, and praying to God to enable me to create change, to change things that were in my family as far as the conditions. I didn't understand society at the time, but it just seemed like poor people were just born to be poor and remain poor until they died."

I sense that Peewee had not planned to say these things. But something in the moment, as perfect and fragile as a bubble, suspends us all. The room is still. Little Peewee looks at his father with learning eyes. Children, when there is no reason to do otherwise, accept, unexamined, a parent's sheltering love as an article of nature, absent any knowledge of the road traveled to provide it.

"We was very happy as a family, happy as a family could be because the condition we lived in wasn't good. You never really saw carpet or nothing. It was always linoleum. We never really knew about a color TV, because the black-and-white was the only TV in the house. I think when you're young, you're more concerned with the affection that's in the family. And because the affection was as strong between the family as a unit, that other realities didn't seem to matter as much until you started becoming older and becoming more aware of your surroundings and your conditions."

His expression alters, almost imperceptibly, and then recovers, as if he has been taken backwards by an unwanted memory.

"I was angry, angry at the conditions I was living under, angry at the fact that you had to keep shaking the cereal box in the morning so the roaches would go to the bottom, angry at you knew how other people was living, and other people had cars, and other people had things, and angry at the fact that you couldn't see ahead, you couldn't see a future, you couldn't talk about a future. You couldn't see anything.

"My mother loved us. She worked so hard. I used to observe my father, and I had so much respect for him, because I was *with* my father. He drank often and died later in life of cirrhosis of the liver. But the thing I respected most about him is the fact that he never, ever, physically hit my mother. And I saw times when he would get mad and angry about different things. He'd leave and come back three or four days later, but he would never ever physically hit my mother.

"So, when I was twelve, I began a life of crime. I did it to try to figure out a way to secure a future for my family. I can remember nights at times being in Lewisburg prison, and the only thing that made any kind of sense was the fact that I could look at it and say, well, you know, at least I was able to do the things I did to make sure that my children would never have to worry about the life of crime and living the wrong way."

Keep it real. This is real. Nose scraping across a hard cement pavement. Close. Ugly close. *There* is here.

"Child and Furious and others listen to me because they know I've been where they were, and millions still are . . . God knows I have. . . ."

4

DÉJÀ VU

Virginia Colony
1640

In 1640, Anthony Johnson owned 250 acres of farmland along the Pungoteague Creek in Northampton County of the Virginia Colony. Johnson, his wife, Mary, and their four daughters were black. Like the large majority of Europeans in the colony, Johnson, an African from Angola, had earlier been purchased under an indenture contract to work as a servant for a set number of years. At the time of Johnson's arrival around 1620, the laws of the Virginia Colony did not contemplate slavery, but only the status of indentured or contract servantship. Johnson had become a free man, like all the others, upon fulfillment of the terms of his contract.

Johnson had every reason in 1640 to feel secure. He owned his own home. He enjoyed all the privileges that belonged to free Englishmen in the colony. He employed workers, at least some of whom were white. By all historical accounts, he was treated like any other planter. He and four hundred other blacks among the nineteen thousand Virginia settlers took comfort (if they gave it any thought at all) as baptised Christians that under English law they could not be enslaved for life.

From its inception, the colony had been met with one crisis after another. In 1609, there were five hundred settlers. By the spring of 1610, only sixty remained alive. Their ranks had been decimated by disease and famine. And inasmuch as the English settlers believed themselves to have the God-given right to impose English law on anyone, including the indigenous First Americans, the colonists gratuitously aroused the ire of a people with whom they might have established a more cooperative relationship.

Anthony Johnson had survived it all: disease, famine, and even an Indian attack on the Bennett plantation where he had been satisfying the terms of his indenture contract.

By 1640, the Virginia colony and Anthony Johnson were flourishing. Virginia planters like Johnson were exporting sixty thousand pounds of tobacco per year back to England. Everything seemed to be going well save the original plan to meet all labor needs through contracted indentureship. Cheap labor was increasingly becoming hard to come by.

That same year, three Virginia servants broke their indenture contracts and ran away to Maryland: a Scotsman named James Gregory, a Dutchman named Victor, and a black named John Post. All three were apprehended and returned to Virginia to stand trial. The Scotsman and the Dutchman each received a sentence of thirty lashes, a year's extension of his indenture, and three years of extended service to the colony.

As for John Post, the black, who had been tried for the same offense as the two whites, the Jamestown court ordered that "he shall serve his master or his assigns for the time of his natural life." Since the establishment of this, the first permanent English colony in America, no white had ever received such a sentence. The auguries of what lay ahead had taken form.

In 1641, Massachusetts became the first English colony to recognize racial slavery. The other colonies, from the north to the south, would follow in its train. To be black in America would henceforth mean to be a slave. The prosperous Johnsons would never again be secure.

Malone, New York
2000

Before 1986, Malone, a small town nestled in a pine-flecked plateau of the New York State north country, had been in deep trouble. Once called the Star of the North, the all-white (with the exception of a black deaf mute the towners called Snowball) town of ten thousand had fallen on hard economic times. On Main Street, the old Flanagan Hotel, where "Dutch" Schultz, the mobster, had flamboyantly boarded during his '33 tax evasion trial, stood shuttered.

The J. J. Newberry factory had closed. Sears Roebuck and Company had also called it quits. The dairy farms had collapsed. A rusting rail junction lay all but idle, mocking the old-timers' reminiscences. A shadow of defeat draped like a pall. The town, mourning, made little sound, its inhabitants waiting hollow-eyed like desperate millers for grist.

Shortly before, in jurisdictions across the country, lawmakers had begun to criminalize nonviolent drug use with resolve enough to make prophets of the paranoids who spied in the politicians' veiled deliberations an unarticulated plan to re-suscitate the moribund economies of rural hamlets like Ma-lone. Grist to render the miller merry. Black grist, brown grist, time immemorial, makes the best bread for maw America.

In New York State, under the so-called Rockefeller drug laws, a first-time nonviolent drug offender would be sentenced to a fifteen-year term in a state prison. Lawmakers, state and local, had written the tedious language with devilish care and meticulous foresight. Spanky-spanky for this infraction, the rack for that. Powder and crack, white and black. The law-makers knew their markets well enough. When the dragnet brought home its harvest, not surprisingly, the ensnared, newly marketable chattel turned up overwhelmingly black and brown.

Thus, the boom that saved little white Malone began. The music of national rural resurgence: bluegrass and construction cranes. An old melody with a new lyric. With schools, bridges, rail-beds, hospitals, and sundry other public holdings crumbling of age and neglect, the nation's lawmakers set about building, af-ter 1980, two hundred state and federal prisons to house its booty. Obscure incorporated spaces on the Colorado plains, the Texas panhandle, and the coalfields of eastern Kentucky offered themselves as sites for new prisons. In Missouri, thirty-one road signs vied in a lively competition won by Licking.

Ironically, in New York, Mario Cuomo, a liberal Demo-cratic governor, would precipitate his state's catch-and-cage rural-development juggernaut. In 1980, the state of New York had thirty-three prisons. During the next twenty years, it would build thirty-eight more, virtually all in rural areas. Three of New York's new prisons would be built in Malone. With the prisons would come sixteen hundred new well-paying jobs and, among other things, eighteen new holes for the golf course.

Under the Rockefeller drug laws, New York, an early slave state, would see its prison population triple in a few years.

Calvin Beale, senior demographer, U.S. Department of Agriculture: "If you have a prison come in with fourteen hundred prisoners, you're probably going to get four hundred jobs out of that, and in a rural setting that's a lot of jobs."

By 1986, Malone had finished construction of its three new prisons and, in one fell swoop, by adding five thousand inmates to its census count, qualified for additional state and federal dollars.

When reminded that New York's sentencing policies were discriminatory and harshly unfair, the good citizens of Malone importuned their representatives sitting in the state legislature in Albany to do nothing to slow the flow of inmates to Malone.

According to Robert Gangi, the executive director of the Correctional Association of New York, reform efforts had effectively been defeated by "the vested interests that Republican state senators have in keeping the spigot flowing and keeping the prisoners flowing into the system."

As Malone began to enjoy the lowest unemployment rate it had seen in twenty years, Peewee Kirkland practiced in New York the only entrepreneurship allowed to him. He could not have known how high against him the deck had been stacked.

5

PLAYING THE HAND YOU ARE DEALT

I hadn't thought much about it. I hadn't thought much about anything I hadn't been taught to think much about. I was a child, five years senior to the Peewee Kirkland I would not meet until fifty years later in a function room at Howard University. And even while growing up in segregationist Virginia, like the billions elsewhere who must suffer unjust societies to have them remain ordered, I not only feared the law, I respected it.

Oh, I knew from civics that Virginia's laws were made by men, bad men, white men, racist, bad white men. But I, like most around me, was maneuvered to distinguish the "law" from those who wrote it. The laws of segregation were unfair, yes, but aberrant, I believed, while the spine of the law's corpus had to have been wrought in a high, objective, nearly hallowed place. You see, my thinking was tightly circumscribed, but I did not know or even suspect such at the time.

If I could be caused to root for the cavalry in its defense of "innocent" white settlers against the whooping cinema "savagery of bloodthirsty Indians," I could be manipulated to accept anything, including Tarzan, the near-mute, as king of all Africa.

Wherever one has something (any infinitesimal morsel) to lose, one usually accepts the basic laid-down dispensatory arrangement for goods and privileges, no matter how inequitable the formula. Not without quarrel, mind you, but absent, all the same, any resolve that one might describe as tending toward the insurrectionary. Even the complaints are pro forma, more whimpers of offended dignity than appeals born of expectation.

Virginia treated us bestially. It held us separate and under. It muzzled every expression of our talent. It denied us our story, old and new. It stole for a bitter song the fruits of our labor. It did to us a savage deal more than England had ever done to her first American colony's rebellious white founders. Yet after slavery, at least in the period of my humiliating childhood, violent political revolt never *occurred* to us, and not just because we had considered it and found it infeasible.

Even during the worst of times, we never, in significant numbers, wanted to overthrow anything. All we really wanted was *in*. As *to Xerox* now means *to copy*, in my youth, *Frigidaire* meant *refrigerator*. *Revolution* meant, and only meant, the *American revolution*. Revolution was good.

Revolution was bad. Patrick Henry, a slave owner and hero of the American revolution, was good. John Brown, a fomenter of revolution against slavery, was bad. *Don't even call what the lunatic was planning "revolution."* And so we didn't. Revolution is a good thing. It means only the glorious American revolution. You know, as in *refrigerator* and *Frigidaire*.

Thus controlled, we have not even by now fully fathomed the causes of our long-running social dilemma. Indeed, we *are* depressed over our general bereftness. But we attribute nothing. We assign no thematic responsibility. We take it upon ourselves.

Our room is lightless. The ceiling is impenetrable and low

to our heads. We . . . I . . . simply cannot *see* who has done this to us anymore.

We are angry, but we have not been disposed to make art of the anger. *They* instruct us with power's large voice that anger too is bad. Hence we have not hoisted it on an anthem staff. Not made of it the soaring song of our condition, our cause, our struggle. Not embraced its normalcy, its naturalness. Not assuaged our complex with it. Not braced from its sword. Instead, our poor and dispossessed have been caused to wear their disgraced anger as a soil of defeat.

The room is so dark, the ceiling so low, that anger can only vent horizontally. This, the horizontal kind, is good *anger*, power's larger voice implies. Black sons fall in the streets like flies. Nothing happens. These, the habits of a tacitly praised self-destruction. The new economics of penal grist.

I don't know just when Peewee started along the road to prison. I suppose it was early in his life. He may not know exactly when himself. It can be safely said, however, that it was long before he committed his first crime.

Richard "Peewee" Kirkland was born on May 6, 1945, in Harlem Hospital to Mary and Joseph Kirkland. Mary Kirkland worked in the payroll department at Metropolitan Hospital in Harlem. Joseph Kirkland was a mimeograph operator. Peewee was the couple's second child. The first, Joseph Jr., nicknamed Lionel, had been born the year before Peewee. The family lived in a brownstone walk-up apartment building on 117th Street between Lenox and Fifth. All told, eight people, including a grandmother, Mamie Richards; her sister, Alice Newbold; a brother, Larry (who would arrive ten years later); and a cousin, Marva Richards, the child of Peewee's mother's brother, "Uncle

Chief," lived in six small rooms: four bedrooms, a living room (converted to a bedroom), and a kitchen. The six-story building stood on a corner. There were six families to a floor. The Kirklands lived on the fourth floor.

The building was old and had gone untended by its absentee owners for what seemed a long term of years. The hallways were dark and fetid.

More often than not, the elevator did not work. While their parents were at work, the Kirkland children, not unlike countless others living in Harlem under similar circumstances, routinely sidestepped strangers, bodies slumped, heads lolling, on the stairways and halls connecting the street entrance to the front door of their apartment.

The event that caused Uncle Chief's daughter, Marva, to come and live with the Kirklands changed Peewee, although it was one of many such formative events and was not, when depersonalized, unusual.

When Peewee was little, Sugar Ray Robinson was the middleweight champion of the world. Those who knew about such things called him the greatest pound-for-pound fighter on the planet. Some said the greatest ever. Practically every black man on the face of the earth knew who Sugar Ray Robinson was, liked his style, pantomimed his blazing combinations, envied his looks.

Peewee idolized Sugar Ray, who with his nightclub, sky-blue Cadillac, and scads of adoring women, was the star of Harlem. Peewee idolized Uncle Chief even more than he did Sugar Ray, and Uncle Chief had been a prizefighter too. Legend had it that he had actually beaten Sugar Ray in a fistfight after an argument on the roof of another Harlem brownstone while Sugar Ray was champion of the world. You have never heard of Uncle Chief only because, I am told, he never got the breaks.

Peewee was used to the summer sounds that wafted through the open windows of his family's apartment: the throb of Hollywood mufflers, the coaxing of street vendors, the din of doorstep debate, the hiss of air brakes, the deep, rich warble of Dinah Washington, the occasional pop that might as likely have been a gunshot as a firecracker. But this time Peewee knew immediately that something had gone very wrong. The scream from the sidewalk below had frightened him. It had tailed into an awful keening before Peewee bolted through the apartment door.

He slowed himself at the building's entrance as if to forestall learning the source of the commotion on the sidewalk ten feet below him. He could not see what the growing crowd pushed forward to investigate. A phalanx of uniformed New York City police officers struggled to form itself into a restraining rope. Angry shouts rose. A police officer's service cap was knocked askew.

"Move back! Move back I said!" an officer commanded, his perspiring face reddening. Peewee hesitated, put a foot down on the first step, and then retreated to the stone landing to crane his neck. He could see nothing except the officers and an increasingly restive crowd that had circled from the sidewalk out into the street around a yellow taxicab. The cab was driverless with its driverside and rear rightside passenger doors standing ajar.

"You kilt him. You murdered him. He wasn't doin' nothin'," a man shouted, his angry voice rising above the din of the now noisy crowd.

Peewee came down the steps and stopped to plot a course

through the outer ring of the crowd. An elderly man with a drawn, leathery, dark face turned, looked at him, and averted his eyes. Peewee pushed himself between the man and a young woman he recognized as Sugar Sadie.

The woman who had screamed in an unnatural voice was now sobbing. The sound of grief worked for a moment to temper the crowd's wrath. Then, Peewee recognized the mournful exhalations as his mother's. The crowd parted for him. Through a picket of blue trousers, he saw her on her knees with a wet face, its aspect terrible and turned to the sky, as if it were beseeching explication from an indifferent God.

On the ground before his mother, Peewee saw the still figure of Uncle Chief. It did not look like the Uncle Chief who had taken him to see the Giants play at the Polo Grounds and defeated the middleweight champion of the world on a Harlem rooftop. It did not look like the "dead" bodies Peewee had seen in movies. It bore no resemblance to anything living. Its legs were turned at odd angles, as if to suggest that death had filched not only life, but any chance Uncle Chief might have had to arrange himself in death with lifelike dignity.

The body's unseeing eyes looked straight out from a head framed on the concrete in a widening halo of blood. Peewee stared at the man-sized marionette that had moments before been a favorite uncle emerging from a cab to visit family. Uncle Chief's hands had been in his pants pockets as the two policemen approached. There had been a brief exchange before five bullets ended Uncle Chief's life. His pockets had contained only three quarters, a wallet, and keys.

Peewee was nine years old.

Ever since human beings evolved to foresight, the common darkness that has bound us all is the inexplicableness of life:

where it comes from, alone and unique; where it goes with its departing sigh; indeed, what it is, even. But death, however defiant of explanation, sane societies make efforts to spare their young sight of.

Victims don't recognize milestones. Such is left to ambitious historians.

6

PEEWEE'S REVENGE

Peewee is telling me about Uncle Chief. This is two months after the luncheon. We are talking across a conference table in the Manhattan offices of Pauline Barfield, owner of a black public relations firm and a supporter of Mark Lawrence's Black Male Empowerment Summit.

"I just never saw cops the same. My father used to have a club, you know, a social club, and I knew at nine or ten, I knew what guns and things like that was because my father, they used to have guns in the club, and they used to go on the roof and shoot them. And I remember one time just thinking about that incident from my uncle getting killed by the cop, and I remember sitting one afternoon in the living room on the pullout couch where my grandmother and godmother slept at night."

Alone in the apartment, Peewee rose from the pullout couch and went to the living room window, knowing the cops would be there.

He thought about how Uncle Chief, dead just a week and a half, had liked to call out, coming through the door, "How's my big man." The memory, alloyed with grief, hardened Peewee's resolve.

There were two of them standing on the sidewalk outside the subway entrance at 117ᵗʰ Street and Lenox Avenue. Peewee did not recognize them. Both were white, but there the similarities ended. One was tall, thin, and young and appeared to be feigning appreciation for a joke being theatrically told by his failed-looking, middle-aged partner, whose belt and service revolver were partially obscured by a doughnut of draping flesh.

From the window four stories up, Peewee could hear the fat patrolman laugh.

Peewee went to the closet and pulled open the door. The top hinge screws had pulled out of the doorframe, causing the toe of the door to deepen the arc it had carved in the ancient linoleum that covered most of the painted surface of the wood floor.

The family's outerwear hung like stage curtains open in the center to reveal two long-barreled rifles that leaned against the closet's back wall. Peewee paused and took a deep breath. His father had sternly admonished him never to touch the guns. Peewee grasped the stouter of the two rifles by the barrel and dragged it toward the living room window with its stock bumping along over the uneven floor. He had never fired or, for that matter, touched a gun before. Trying without success to seat the butt of the stock against his shoulder, he awkwardly pointed the barrel in the general direction of the two patrolmen and jerked on the trigger.

For a moment, Peewee, temporarily deafened and knocked backward into the room, did not know what had happened. Frightened, he dropped the rifle on the floor, stumbled over it, and approached the window from the side, hiding as much of himself from view as he could.

The patrolmen, unharmed, had taken cover inside the subway stairwell. The young one had lost his cap scrambling down the stair. Peewee saw the officer's head slowly rise from the well until the man's eyes were just above the street surface. The patrolman's head turned slowly and stopped, facing toward Peewee's building. Stiffened with fear, Peewee flattened himself against the wall and waited.

Within minutes, sirens and tire squeals signaled the arrival of a small army of uniformed policemen. Peewee remained motionless. Nothing in the room moved except the frayed lace curtains that rode a mild breeze in and out of the open window.

Peering through the curtain from a near-flat angle, Peewee could see nine policemen on the rooftops of the other side of 117th Street. All nine were crouched over with their service revolvers drawn.

In the hours that followed, the police searched with binoculars from every roof and scoured on foot every building on Peewee's block. But no one ever knocked at the door of the Kirkland apartment where nine-year-old Peewee leaned rigidly against a wall watching afternoon shadows slowly lengthen across a linoleum floor.

After what seemed an endless term, Peewee recognized the noises of retreat. He waited a measure more before dragging the rifle back to the closet and placing it against the wall as it had been before. He lifted the door slightly by the knob, freeing its toe from the flooring, and pushed it shut.

"I never told my mother. I didn't never tell anybody. I never told anybody because my father was real strict. I didn't know what kind of rifle it was, but I knew it was loaded. I expected it to fire when I pulled the trigger, but not as loud as it did. I didn't expect that. It scared me to death."

I ask if he meant to hit one of the policemen.

"I don't think I did. You know, I think I just wanted to just shoot it in their direction, at them."

They were looking for him. *They* were looking for him before he was born. In bygone eras whose passing he had no knowledge of. *They* looked for him among the brave Maroons who had fled sugarcane fields for the refuge of Jamaica's Blue Mountains. *They* looked for him in the tall grass of Africa's savanna and in the hot, humid shadow of her glorious rain forest.

They had hounded him for so long now. In the black reek of Gorée's chamber. In the cramped, diarrheal space joining the dead to the living on de Wolf family ships. Through two and a half American centuries of human bondage. Through swamp and bayou. En route anywhere to anything upright—to read, to work, to own, to vote, to remember, to dream, to be. *They* were looking for him. As always.

He had not known that twenty thousand years thence a forebear in Congo had inscribed a bone with formulae Western mathematicians would later attest to be the foundation of modern mathematics. He never thought about such things. He could not learn them under his burden. How could he have believed such things in any case? He could scarcely think of anything beyond surviving. He was young and small and tired and *blind*. But *we* were blind as well and could see neither him nor the conditions that had befallen him now and before.

Their seven-hundred-year-old strategy was brilliant for its simplicity: *if you want the horse to pull the wagon, first put blinders on it.*

Thus *they* were looking for him still. In job-starved African cities. On dying Caribbean banana farms. On the new American public and private prison plantations. On the corner of 117th Street and Lenox Avenue in Harlem.

They were looking for him to feed *their* children. He meant nothing to them personally. But the economic system needed him as a statistic, a faceless, blinkered datum on which to pivot resources, to realize the growth masters' success by a factor of however many of them it would profit to catch him, keep him, work him, stud him, mash him like a blind ant.

As it had been for seven centuries, *they* would train him as they hunted him; train him to know that he would always and only list among the ranks of the hunted. And thus behave.

New York senator Daniel Patrick Moynihan would call the behavior "speciation." *Washington Post* columnist David Broder, approving of the senator's *science*, would define *speciation* to mean "the impending creation of a different kind of human, one raised outside a father-mother setting."

Two centuries ago, similar exculpatory analysis had been wrought by whites to describe the slaves upon whose backs the economic might of white America was being constructed.

Yesterday is today. In the year 2001, at home and abroad, blacks, disproportionately, are seen by the masters of the American economy as little more than human compost for America's continued global dominance.

They had been looking for Peewee for a long time, though he was only nine years old.

7

THE ASPIRING
AMERICAN
ENTREPRENEUR

I do not pay much attention to anything in the room other than the table and the tiny Sony tape recorder that stands on it between us like a blinking witness. The walls are lined with shelves containing reports of New York State court decisions. Peewee and I are literally surrounded by law. I nearly laugh aloud at the irony but suppress the urge. I had spent three years of my life studying law under high-minded professors at the Harvard Law School. (The Harvard people always insert the reverence-inducing *the* before the law school's name.) Peewee had spent at least half of his life contriving to make a fool of the law. Risking getting ahead of myself here, both of us failed.

As to discerning its real purpose, the shiny philosophical symbols of American law had blinded one of us and trapped the other. A small personal illustration: Like most, I had been impressed by Harvard Law School and never suspected it of hiding in plain view a sordid provenance. (Harvard Law School had been endowed by its founder, Isaac Royall, through the sale of black Caribbean sugar-plantation slaves. Representing this founding transaction on the school's crest are three bushels of Antiguan sugarcane shown under the banner word *veritas* against a blood-red field.)

Like those of so much of America's private and public institutional edifice, Harvard's roots are buried in shame. But shame long shed is a face that modern privilege never wears. For privilege hides in gilded comfort behind timeworn and sturdy doors. One such door is American law, which invariably protects first the interests of those who write it. In its oldest core expression, law itself is the Great American Discriminator, the wondrous cloak and consecrator of unfairly gained, lopsided wealth. For only *after* the mayhem, *after* an era of untaxed robber-baronism, *after* 246 years of uncompensated bondage, *after* a century of economic and social racial discrimination, *after* greed-based black codes, restrictive covenants, peonage laws, lynchings and pogroms—*after,* and only *after* all this, did the great door of "justice" grind shut finally on the odious acts and, in one irreversible, time-sweeping arc, preserve both the ill-gotten wealth of America's white criminal gentry and the planned poverty of its centuries-old black victims.

"I started staying out at night at a young age." Peewee looks up at the ceiling as he says this. He has taken himself back into the streets.

"I was about eleven or twelve. I used to carry groceries, and then I started opening cab doors downtown."

I ask him where the grocery market was and who owned it.

"It was across the street from where we lived. It was a big store. It was owned by white people."

I ask him what the owners were. Italian, German, Jewish?

"I don't know. I didn't know the difference between white people. White people were white people."

I ask him why he went downtown to open cab doors.

"You opened a door, they'd give you a tip.

"I used to sell newspapers at night, which didn't end up good, because what happened was in doing that, that put me in a position at like twelve years old to be out there. And being out there, I just through a friend of mine named Billy Blaze, who was three years older than me . . ."

Peewee stops and thinks, his face blank. Then he smiles inside a memory and continues.

"Billy was my running buddy and he was kind of like fast. He really knew how to gamble real well, and he taught me how to gamble. He was also tough as nails."

I start to form a picture of Billy Blaze but think to check it with Peewee so that I can make an accurate record of both the events and the participants to them. Peewee said that Billy was "real light-skinned, curly hair. He was sort of like what they would consider a gorgeous black person. But Billy hated that about himself. He hated his hair. He hated the fact that he was light-skinned. He used to always say that, you know what I mean?"

Peewee's voice trails off. I have formed a new picture of Billy Blaze, but I am still having trouble seeing Peewee and his friend as twelve- and fifteen-year-olds. The mind's eye resolves the imagined images into older faces. I tell myself, *This Billy is only fifteen*, and ask a logical question.

"Was Billy in school? Did he work?"

Peewee smiles again but this time it is a *what-planet-is-he-from* smile.

"Billy was a hustler. He didn't go to school." I knew and didn't know what a hustler did in the same way that I knew and didn't know what an arbitrageur or a stockbroker or a currency speculator did. Feeling a bit stupid, I ask, "What exactly does a hustler do?"

"Well, you just be out there, and you learn how to survive in the street, and Billy knew how to survive. Billy knew how to lend money." *Billy is an investment banker.* "He knew the money game. He was an unbelievable gambler." *Billy is a securities investor.* "He gambled well. And he introduced me to a lot of things. He was the one that taught me how to gamble and how to cheat at gambling." *Billy is the stockbroker who ten years ago sold me a real estate limited partnership.* "He taught me how to cheat at craps."

I am trying to distinguish Billy Blaze from many of the respected businesspeople that I know whose names are the stuff of American legend. They were rich. Billy intended to be. In an economy constructed of goods and services, they produced no goods and a dubious, if not unethical, service. Much the same was true of Billy.

"He taught me. And I was like a quick study, you know what I mean, if it was about trying to figure out a way to get money, and then I'd find myself not going to sell papers although I had built an unbelievable paper route."

Peewee had carried the *New York Daily News.* I ask him how big his route was.

"About seven."

"Seven?"

"Seven."

"You mean seventy?"

"Seven."

"You delivered seven papers?"

"No. No. We used to buy big piles of papers and I had seven guys selling papers. I had guys working for me."

Peewee is an entrepreneur.

"Working for you when you were twelve?"

"Oh, yes, yes, yes. I wasn't doing it. They was selling the papers. So, yes, I had guys . . . I had a young entrepreneur's mind except I didn't realize it."

"And this was all clean?"

"Yes, there was nothing bad. But when they was selling the papers, I was with him."

"Who? Billy Blaze?"

"Yes, with Billy Blaze. He was learning me how to gamble and learning me how to . . ." Peewee punctuates a pause with a mirthless chuckle that dies in a sigh.

I am slightly confused. I like him but I still cannot puzzle him out. Involuntarily, I try to understand his story against the straight line of my own social development.

"Look," I say, "you had a strict father."

"Oh, yes."

"Your father was a good man. Your mother was a good woman. Your parents were together. How did you allow yourself to be influenced by somebody like Billy Blaze?"

"Well, Billy didn't have to influence me. I influenced him."

"Why?"

"Because of change. Because my mind was dead set on making money, becoming successful, and changing the conditions that my family was living under."

"You didn't think it could be done in a legal way?"

"Yes, but that would have took too long to become a reality, and I wasn't as concerned with that as I was with trying to figure out a way and means to change the living conditions that I was living under. So Billy didn't pursue me as much as I pursued Billy. Because Billy would say things like, 'Well, man, you know your father's going to have a fit.' And I'd say things like, 'Yes, I understand, but you know what? He's not going to beat you; he going to beat me.' "

"What kind of stuff was he teaching you?"

"Well, we learned how to take the medallions off cabs. It was cool to take the medallions off the cabs, and I was a kid so I was in situations where they'd do it. I was the guy on watch, standing on the corner, making sure if the police came. And we would take the medallions and sell them for like ten thousand or fifteen thousand dollars. People didn't really know how valuable they were. I think at the time they might have been worth fifty thousand or sixty thousand dollars. But we would just sell them, and that was a lot of money."

"Did the buyers know that they were hot medallions?"

"Yes, they knew, but didn't care. They just wanted them. And it grew from that to jewelry stores and I would play a major role at that point."

Billy Blaze, Nervous Sonny, and Blue Juice stood on the sidewalk with Peewee across the street from the store in the Diamond District on Forty-seventh Street between Fifth and Sixth Avenues. It was a scalding early-August afternoon. Peewee, thirteen and a head shorter than the three others, who were three years older than he, found some relief from the blast of the sun in Billy's shadow. They stood there for a good while and watched the two large glass display windows that framed the store's entryway. The sidewalks were teeming with people. The four boys took no pains to hide themselves. Remembering his assignment, Peewee focused on the store's twin glass doors, whose two stainless-steel handles looked like praying hands from where he stood.

Billy looked at Peewee and nodded. Peewee picked up a burlap satchel that strained around its blocky content, walked to the corner, and waited for the light to change. Billy, Nervous Sonny, and Blue Juice followed fifteen feet behind.

Peewee crossed Forty-seventh Street and moved along the sidewalk towards the entrance to the store. Seventy feet from the twin doors, Peewee slowed and drew a breath to settle his nerves. Upon reaching the doors, Peewee put the satchel down and removed from it a pair of handcuffs, with which he joined the praying-door handles together. He then drew from the satchel two bricks.

Inside the store, the proprietor, his son, and three customers heard two loud reports from shattering glass. The proprietor, a balding, middle-aged white man with sagging jowls and deepening worry lines, ill advisedly rushed to the doors but could not open them. The store's three customers (a well-dressed black professional woman and two white men in business suits) looked for guidance to the proprietor's son, whose face bore a near silly look of perpetual surprise. For an age of seconds, the proprietor exerted himself futilely against the doors as his son and the customers watched Billy Blaze, Blue Juice, and Nervous Sonny rake gemstones into bags through the shattered glass windows.

"We didn't understand the stones we were grabbing, but we did know from the person who set it up, because there was always people setting everything up, that there was gemstones. A lot of jewelry was gemstones, which caused me to learn the diamond business real fast, because I wanted to understand the value of what we was selling and if we was getting robbed, so I learned the diamond business by the time I was like fifteen. I knew the diamond business better than most jewelers. I knew color stones better than jewelers, because most jewelers just know stones, but I knew color stones. I knew sapphires, rubies, because I used to own a jewelry store, me and an Italian."

A meeting had been arranged with the two Italians at an Automat on Forty-second Street. The meeting had become necessary after the agreed-upon price of $300,000 for the jewelry had not been paid by the Italians. Blue Juice's father, who was known as the Books, knew the Italians because they "banked his numbers." The Books had turned over the jewelry to the Italians shortly after the robbery. The teenagers knew also that the Italians, if not "made men," were in one way or another connected to the Mafia. Weeks had gone by and . . . nothing. Billy had said to Blue Juice, "We love you and that's your father, but somebody's got to pay this money." And so the Books had arranged a face-to-face of four black kids (one, thirteen, and three, sixteen) on a pleather booth seat across a Formica table from two Italian guys in sharkskin suits.

Peewee, seated next to Billy, pulled himself forward onto the shoulder of the seat to rest his arms on the table. The Italians and all of the boys except Peewee were carrying. Billy spoke for the group.

"You agreed to three hundred thousand dollars for our jewelry. Where is our money? What's going on here, man?"

"Look, I gotta tell yuh, somethin' happened," said the younger Italian, who looked about thirty-five. "Look, it's our fault, right?" He held both palms up in false supplication. "I can't explain it, you know, but that's how come we couldn't pay you."

"What you mean you can't pay us? You got our shit, man," said Billy, standing right up to the Italian guy.

Then the Italian guy said, "You don't understand."

Billy said, "Well, make me understand, man. How are you going to pay us?"

"Well," said the Italian guy, "we can give you nine hundred thousand dollars' worth of drugs. Or we can give you three hundred thousand dollars' worth of drugs and you can make nine hundred thousand dollars off it. And instead of getting three hundred thousand dollars, you'd be getting nine hundred thousand dollars."

Peewee tells me across the conference table:

"Now we're sitting there . . . Because I understand money, because at the time I had one hundred thousand dollars myself in cash from medallions and playing craps. I had it stashed at my older brother's house. All of us, you know, had cash stashed at different people's houses. We used to set up once in a while in Harlem, because Billy knew craps real well. I think we split over one hundred thousand dollars apiece. It was a gambling hall in the city that everybody used to go to, right? What we did was go to the gambling hall at night and put magnets down up under the gambling table. And when they come back the next day to gamble, Billy won like maybe six hundred thousand dollars. But it was because of the magnets. They was under the craps table, and there was a thing, and if you click it, every time you click it, because the magnet was on it, it would turn. If somebody had a number six, every time you clicked it, it went to seven, so they lost. The only way you could tell about the special dice was to put them in water. They would go down. If you put the regular dice in water, they wouldn't. But, you see, the dice we was using was our dice. And that night we won more than six hundred thousand dollars from hustlers, man, at a place called the Big House. The hustlers didn't have the slightest idea 'cause one of the first things that Billy taught me is that the easiest person to cheat is a hustler. He's the last person in the world that think somebody's going to cheat him.

"Well, anyway, I'm thirteen and sitting there across from these two Italians and I'm sort of like dumbfounded for two reasons. One, I don't understand how to turn three hundred thousand dollars into nine hundred thousand dollars, and the other reason is because I never wanted to be involved with drugs. You just see what drugs do to the community, how it decays the community. So, I never really wanted to be involved."

Billy looked across at the two Italian guys and after a while said, "Okay," and that was that.

On the street outside the Automat, Peewee looked at Billy, Blue Juice, and Nervous Sonny. They looked happy about the meeting's outcome.

Peewee said to Billy, "Man, I don't understand. They robbing us. Why would we go along with this?"

Billy said, "Look here, man, if we don't go along with this, they're not going to pay us. Anyway, we might be able to turn the drugs into forty to one. You know what we could do with that?"

They knew the game and were explaining it to Peewee, who, at thirteen, was still a trainee.

"Man, all we got to do is give it to Bo Tree," Blue Juice said. Bo Tree was a black man involved in drugs who got high himself.

Peewee says now, "So I'm listening, and it happened, and

they ended up making a move and giving it to Bo, and not only that it wasn't nine hundred thousand dollars we made, but more like two million dollars before it was over. My cut was somewhere between three hundred thousand and four hundred thousand dollars because I got mine first because I said, 'Man, you know what, man? I don't know if this is a good move. What's going to happen is we going to get involved in this shit, and the next thing you know, nobody's going to get nothing out of it.' So they said, 'Well, I'll tell you what we'll do, man. You'll get your money off the top.' So, that meant I'd get my money first.

"Oh, another thing. The Italians never did explain what happened other than the fact that they was just trying to straighten it and make it right, which later in life I learned something, what really happened. And what really happened was they sold the jewelry for exactly what they wanted to sell it for but didn't want to give us the money."

After the boys robbed their second jewelry store, Peewee was approached on 125th Street by a pleasant, well-dressed white man who looked to be in his late forties. "The people who run the jewelry store two blocks down want to talk to you."

Peewee looked up at him, measuring him. Wary. "Talk to me about what?"

The man's eyes narrowed above a faint, knowing smile. "Look. Here's the number. The owner's name is Goldstein. Call him."

Peewee looked at him and said nothing. The man's face opened into a *I-know-and-you-know-I-know* toothy grin. "Look. What can you lose by calling the guy? Right?"

Peewee closed a fist around the card the man pressed into his hand.

Peewee waited two days before calling the number from a pay phone on the street two blocks from his home.

Diffident. "Hel . . . hello, may I speak to Mr. Goldstein."

"Which one?" The voice was phlegmy and used-up.

"I, I don't know. Some white guy on the street say Goldstein want to talk to me."

"Talk to who?"

"Peewee. My name is Peewee Kirkland."

Silence.

Peewee heard a well-modulated voice in the background and then the sound of a cash register. "You there, man?" More confident now that the disembodied voice had broken off.

"Say you come meet with me," said the liquid voice, lower now, "I'll make it worth your while."

"This ain't no freaky shit, is it?"

"No, nothing like that," said the voice, offended now.

The sign read *Goldstein and Goldstein*, with the *n* in *and* stylized into a diamond. *Jeweler to Harlem, Est. 1927.*

Peewee sat in one of two oak desk chairs amidst boxes that cluttered the store's back room. Abraham Goldstein sat in the other in front of a battered rolltop desk. He was in his late seventies with sunken gray eyes that seemed to sight the end of all things with wry welcome. His shoulders were turned down and in, as if shaped over time by the old chair whose back curved around into brittle and ungraceful arms. His pale gray skin had the texture of a collapsed soufflé. From a part just above his left ear, three bands of white tendrils an inch or so apart stretched across a sepulchral skull finding purchase in an oily spot behind his right ear.

"What's this about?" began Peewee, endeavoring to take charge.

Goldstein's chest rattled as he smiled from memory of his own hardscrabble youth. "I know about you," he said quietly.

"What chu mean? You don't know nothin' about me, man." Not angry, but slow, measured.

"Oh, yes. You and your friends have been robbing jewelry stores."

Goldstein looked at Peewee. Peewee stared at Abraham Goldstein and said nothing.

Peewee remembered what Billy Blaze had taught him about the value of silence. *Billy say, leave a space, man. Sometimes, just don't say nothing. Let the other motherfucka talk until he fuck up.*

The silence lengthened.

A young man, whose voice bore the inflection of higher education, came through the door from the showroom without knocking, "Dad . . . Oh, excuse me, I'm sorry."

"Leave me be for a while, Seth," Goldstein said, and his son quietly closed the door.

The old man paused and locked his forearms down on the armrests as if to affirm a decision he had reached.

"I want you and your friends to rob my store."

"What?"

"I said, I want you and your friends to rob my store, except not just the display windows, but everything in the store."

Peewee didn't have to remember Billy's advice about the value of silence. He didn't quite know what to say in any case.

"What you want us to do that for?"

"That doesn't concern you."

97

"What do we get out of this?"

"You get all the jewelry, all the cash, you can carry out of here. But no guns. You won't need them. I'll let you know the time and day to do it."

"No, no, no. We ain't walking into no setup, man. I look crazy to you? I don't know you. I ain't never seen you before I walked in here five minutes ago."

They paused in mutual retreat.

"Look . . ." Goldstein's voice was weary. "Just rob the goddamn store, all right? You can't lose. We won't push the alarm or call the police until long after you're gone. If you come any morning just after we open at ten, no customers will be here. Any Monday. Any Monday is like that." Goldstein seemed to sag.

Another silence.

"Allst I can say is I ain't listening to nothing you saying until you say why you want us to do this."

Goldstein muttered something unintelligible.

"What?" asked Peewee.

"I said *insurance*. I got to get from under this place. My son doesn't want it and I can't sell it for a fair price. I'm trapped." *Trapped*, Goldstein had said to Peewee, and looked at the thirteen-year-old while feeling indefinably silly.

"I don't know about this deal, man. We have to think about this."

"I don't understand what your problem is. You can't lose on a setup like this." Peewee's eyes narrowed. Goldstein gave him an avuncular look. "Look, I'm sorry. It was a bad choice of words."

"It seem to me we be taking all the risk, man."

"I don't understand." Goldstein was feeling ugly negotiating with a child.

"S'pose you cross us. Who gon' take our word you in on it?"

"Why would I do something like that?"

Peewee thought the question warranted a Billy Blaze silence.

After a period, Peewee said, "I'll talk to my boys about this, but I tell you right now, we got to have somethin' more than jewels and cash."

"What?"

"Maybe somethin' plus a check."

"A check?"

"Yeah, a check."

"But I could stop payment on a check," said Goldstein, incredulous.

"But that ain't why we want you to make a check out to us," said Peewee, watching understanding dawn on Goldstein.

"Well, I can't do that. I can't be tied to this."

"You gon' have to give up somethin' else to make this a fair deal. Way it is, you get the insurance money and no risk. We get the jewels, cash, and all the risk. Shit, we don't have to talk to nobody to get that kin'a deal with less risk 'cause they don't know we comin'."

"Well, you discuss it with your friends and tell me how much this is going to cost me."

"Okay. I be back tomorrow. Then you got to tell me what kin'a jewels will be in the store and how much cash will be in the cash register."

After Peewee had left through a rear exit, Seth knocked lightly, came in, and sat where Peewee had sat.

"How'd it go. Did he buy it?"

"Yeah, I think so. We'll know tomorrow. He has to speak to his colleagues." The old man sounded sincere and ironic all at once.

"Did you tell him about the other store owners?"

"No, that wouldn't have worked. He thinks I'm doing this because I'm desperate to get out. They can find out about the other owners after this goes through."

Peewee says now, "After we had robbed two stores, the people in the Diamond District knew what was going on. They just didn't know how to stop it. The third store we robbed was a setup. The jewelry store set it up, and the fourth time it happened and the fifth time it happened, it was a setup. They set it up for us to do it, and they got the insurance money. I know they was setups because they set it up with me. That's how I ended up in the diamond business."

Goldstein and Goldstein continued in business long after the robbery and the insurance settlement that followed it.

8

PEEWEE'S FATHER

I interrupt Peewee's testament to flip the microcassette and check the batteries. We have been talking for more than two hours without a break. Something is bothering me. A small scratch of inchoate doubt. Or nearer to its proper mark, a mildly disturbing disequilibrium that may be more revealing of me than of Peewee. I have been using *my* math to sum *his* columns, the assumptions of *my* socialization to understand *his* experience. It is not working. I am either naïve or cynical. I cannot be both at the same time. But I cannot know which condition is warranted by truths that seem, more than ever, fluid and relative. I am finding it hard to believe what he is telling me, but believing it nonetheless. It is as if I were living in a house I thought sturdy, if not sumptuous, only to sustain a blow to the blithe spirit upon discovering broad rot at its foundation. If Peewee is being honest with me, there have to be at least two black Americas, Peewee's not only being foreign to mine, but larger than mine as well.

He has told me with fervor that most of the black kids he knew as a child in Harlem were involved in lives of crime:

"There was no other way. There was the ones that got caught and the ones that didn't get caught."

I start the tape and pursue this course. I had been, in light of our discussion, a relatively sheltered child in segregated Richmond, Virginia, when Peewee was robbing jewelry stores in Harlem. I had not known of *any* thirteen-year-old robbers, while Peewee had come to view his early line of criminal work as neighborhood de rigueur. I start from my old assumptions about education as a universally accepted path out. He regards me with wonderment.

"That's not a realistic dream, especially back then. You dream about things but you never knew anybody it happened to. It seemed like it was always meant for the poor to be poor, the middle class to be middle class, and the rich to be rich. You grew up like that and you looking for a way out. Even sublimi- nally you're looking for a way out. And you don't care almost what it takes or what you have to do to create that way out.

"Because also I am thinking about not only my family, but I'm thinking at some point in time I'm going to have a family, and some point in time I'm going to want to raise my family. At some point in time, I'm going to want my kids to go to the bet- ter schools, to have the better things, to live in the nice places. And you find yourself taking chances. In the street they call it throwing bricks.

"If you give a kid a choice, you give a kid a chance. If you don't give a kid a choice, then he going to take chances. And there wasn't no choices. There wasn't no clearly defined choices at all. Even getting an education. Well, so what? I didn't know nobody that had an education I could say, well, because of his education he's this or because of his education he's that."

From the beginning, Peewee loved basketball. He was good,

very good, soon after he began playing. Before reaching his midteens, he could go to his right or to his left with equal facility. He was a natural point guard, a magician with the ball in either dexterous hand. In the language of basketball, he *saw* the whole court, ran the break, and dished off with unerring no-look passes as if he had a hoops sextant seated in his brain stem. His playground friends conferred upon him prodigy status. Grown men allowed him to play with them. Crowds gathered to see the small boy perform moves effortlessly that veteran practitioners of the art could neither learn nor imagine. Unlike the vast majority of those who doggedly pursue mastery of the game, Peewee's craft was not of a piece with the plodders. His was genius. A gift from God. A bequest from King Midas. Genetic munificence. Whatever.

None of this was lost on Peewee. Early on, he believed basketball to be his only legitimate way out of a world that had all but finished shaping him.

At the age of eight he had been playing for two years when his father came to watch him on an outdoor court near Lenox Avenue and 120th Street. It was November, just before Thanksgiving and unseasonably cold. The sky was brilliant and clear but for thin wafers of fast-moving clouds that drifted past like high, white smoke. It was a pickup game, three on three. Peewee, the smallest and youngest of the players, wore a cumbersome mackinaw and street shoes. Still, his gift could be discerned in the subtlest of his motions.

With a medium-range jumper from the right side, Peewee won the game that his father watched.

"Peewee, Peewee," his father called. "Come on. I need you to go with me."

"Okay," Peewee called back, saying, "I'll see you guys

later," to the other players, whose heads were haloed by the cold-weather vapor of breath and perspiration.

"Good Lord, boy, you're gonna be somethin' special," his father said to Peewee as they headed toward the intersection of Lenox and 120th.

Peewee was euphoric when he stepped off the curb to cross Lenox Avenue holding his father's hand. A green and white, Ford Crown Victoria, hardtop convertible pulled across the crosswalk and blocked their path. The passengerside door opened and Peewee heard what sounded to him like a backfiring car engine. As the car's door closed and rubber squealed, Peewee felt his father's hand tear away from his as the slightly built man was blown backward onto the sidewalk from which the two had only moments ago stepped.

"Daddy, Daddy!" Peewee screamed, running toward where his father lay on his back with his black leather jacket open, his hands clutching the right side of his abdomen. A crowd had begun to gather around the boy kneeling beside his father. Peewee saw blood leaking through his father's fingers. "Somebody help him, somebody help him," said Peewee over and over, not knowing what else to do. Tears washed over a brave, shivering lip.

"Call an ambulance," someone said.

Peewee's father, grimacing in pain, spoke for the first time. "No, don't call no ambulance." He then gripped Peewee's arm and pleaded with the boy, "Help me up. I can't go to no hospital. Help me up and help me get home."

The bullet had taken a clean course through Joseph Kirkland's body, touching no vital organs. He did not go to the hospital and remained in the apartment on 117th Street for several weeks until he recovered.

"I didn't know why he didn't go to the hospital, but I found out later why," Peewee says. "He can't go to the hospital because what happens is when it's that kind of situation where bullets go to ballistics, ballistics lead to people. Even if he didn't tell, they'd think he did. I realized all that later but I didn't understand it then."

As I talk to Peewee in a conference room in a Manhattan office building, I harbor nettlesome insecurities about my competence to tell this story, to have you grasp its full implication for black people, indeed for the society in general, with all the intellectual and emotional force of its elemental significance. I hope you will forgive the irrepressible essayist in me, but I think at this point context is needed.

As I listen to Peewee, I extrapolate in my head from his story by a factor of what? Millions like Peewee? I can't say with empirical precision. But anyone with a modicum of sense knows the number is high enough to make the devil blanch. I was never one to write (even had I the requisite aptitude) in the language of arcane symbolism. The story I am being told and am laboring to tell you is important quite bluntly because American society is mass-producing Peewee's developmental experience at an exponentially faster clip than it is mine. It is deeply disturbing that Peewee's story is so commonplace. But it is indeed more frightening that I had not known this and, I suspect, neither had you. Thus, the story could seem compelling simply for its foreignness to your experience. Such is forgivable. But should that be as far as your understanding takes you, you will have missed the better part of the point, as it would appear that much of contemporary black leadership has.

A few clues. During the last twenty years, the state of California has spent more than $5 billion building and expanding twenty-three prisons, while during the same span of time, only one new university was built from the ground up. Such misguided public-spending priorities are consistent with national trends.

We are allowing poverty, and all its attendant pathologies, to fester and replicate out of public policy sight and, thus, out of mind. Neither George W. Bush nor Al Gore made these issues a priority in the 2000 presidential campaign. This notwithstanding, in its quadrennial rite of unrequited affection, the black community awarded Gore more than ninety percent of its votes. Ever reflexive, in New York State, black voters gave Senator Hillary Clinton more than ninety-three percent of their votes before she deleted poverty reduction from her list of top policy priorities altogether.

The coarse, open grain of our social culture suggests that one cannot rise and lift at the same time. To rise, by any means, is wonderfully American. To lift is a loser's obsession. I see the political cartoon in my head. The bemedaled old pol, his ruddy cheeks pinked with termless privilege, his arms open and stretched to the heavens in theatrical thanksgiving for "the greatest republic ever, anywhere," his corpulent butt parked cherry athwart the overdue fault line of a grossly unfair society. He can count. But only beans, money, votes, honorary degrees, and invitations to the White House. His is *success math*, which is more important than *Chicago Math*. He cannot count seismometers. He cannot see cancer cells. He cannot feel pain that is not his own. He believes the gentle rumbling beneath his bottom is caused by a generous serving of pâté he has eaten for lunch at Café Laruche on Thirty-first Street. He is rising but not under his own power. The sound of the explosion is awful, a maddening roar laced with the indelicate language of social anomie and spuming rage.

"Oh dear. Oh dear," bleats the discombobulated old pol, his medals jangling out "America, the Beautiful."

Is not truth ignored, truth nonetheless? Is it no less alive than the distant, unseen star? Does it not, for all its disregard, enjoy an integrity unto itself, as indomitable as the mauve blossom of a lone wildflower on a baked desert plain? Does not such truth survive even in the cold, bleak backside shadow of the instant culture's acting god, at whose resplendent court celebrity plays the jester, the sugary flavor of the moment?

Truth. Is there ever some devil in its detail that affects our sight?

The bemedaled old pol had gone to hundreds, if not thousands, of receptions during his long career in the U.S. Congress.

"Chivas, if you have it," he would always say to the silent black bartender. And the black bartender always *would* have it, and in supplies ample enough to paint roses on the veiny cheeks of the old pol, who had earlier, on the day of his most recent Chivas reception, supported a successful push in the U.S. Congress, since signed into law, barring American students with drug convictions (who were incidentally disproportionately black and Hispanic) from ever receiving any federal aid or student loans to attend college.

Ah . . . truth. You oft-impostered, oft-disowned perfect child. Scotch, cocaine, wine, crack. All choreographers of the altered state. All drugs between which natural morality can draw no defensible distinction. Yet, tinkles sweetly the crystal that holds the Chivas and slams mean the steel door that swipes life and opportunity (and voting rights) from the nonviolent drug offender.

Tobacco had its lobby, and its lobby had the Scotch-loving old pol. Crack cocaine could find no such prominent public friend, although powder cocaine fared better than crack. But the difference between tobacco, cocaine, and the others had really nothing at all to do with logic or morality or truth. For truth, the impervious standard, is not the weakling here, is it? The weakling is *we*, the gullible mass schmucks who would not pry open the old pol's door and make him a *democrat*.

What exactly then is a democracy? What are its necessary elements? What qualities combine to lend it its quintessence? To raise it above its ordinary constituents, mystifying its tenant language, ennobling its founders?

Elections. Would the practice of them alone constitute a democracy? No. Elections are a practice, a ritual, that members of a democracy periodically conduct, but elections are not democracy itself. Presumably, one cannot have democracy without elections. But it is just as true that one can have elections without having democracy.

The truth, please. Is America a democracy? Not in the form of its political system. But in its practice, its spirit?

The old pol and all who know him would think the very question impudent, absurd. But, in a democracy, can the machineries of power be so far removed from the poor and the powerless as to make the name by which their system goes, for them, meaningless? A sour farce? Can it be truthfully described as democracy when those who frame decisions are virtually all of one economic class? Or race? Can a relatively homogeneous, unrepresentative selection of *representatives* be realistically expected to faithfully defend the interests of those whose lives are to them as foreign as extraterrestrials? Must minorities—blacks, Latinos, Asians, Native Americans, the poor generally—be more than decorously but fruitlessly represented, heeded even, sometimes? Does the illusion of democracy constitute a growing danger to the elites whose ranks are lessening relative to the unseen, unheard, uncared for? And as for these, the destitute, isn't it dangerous indeed to have them resign themselves to poverty, then further resign themselves to being stepped upon by those amongst them who have not so resigned themselves? Those who rightly or wrongly believe the only way out of their misery to be along the criminal course?

Peewee's father disappeared not long after he recovered from his wounds. His family explained only that his father was "away." Peewee accepted this explanation. Virtually all of his friends' fathers were "away" too. Peewee was too young to estimate accurately how long his father stayed gone. Only years later did he learn it was two years and where his father had been.

9

WADLEIGH JUNIOR HIGH SCHOOL

By the time he was thirteen, Peewee's senior colleagues in the "life of crime," Billy Blaze, Blue Juice, and Nervous Sonny, had developed complete confidence in his abilities.

"They said, 'Well, man, you got a lot of heart, and the one thing about you is that we know you'd never flip over.' So they knew I would never tell. I don't know how they knew it, but I guess people in the streets can judge character. And they was right. I would rather die first, and I guess they picked up on that.

"And they also felt I was lucky, and that I could think better than all of them could think. A couple of times, they was going to do different things, and I said, 'No, no, no, man. That don't make no sense.' And I told them why, and they didn't do it, and the people that did it got busted. So, they knew I had something that I was bringing to the party. They wouldn't do nothing unless I agreed."

The relationship among the boys continued until Peewee finished high school, where Peewee, his special gift notwithstanding, had no time for varsity basketball until his last year.

In any case, school seldom went smoothly for Peewee, in part because he had difficulty accepting authority. Once at Wadleigh

Junior High School, a white gym teacher named Wilbert Smirney asked Peewee, in something that might have seemed the wrong tone, to play baseball. Peewee refused.

Mr. Smirney said, "I want you to hit the ball, Peewee."

"I don't want to play, Mr. Smirney."

"Well, go ahead! Go ahead! Go ahead!" insisted Mr. Smirney, now angry and uncertain how to handle what now amounted to a challenge to his authority.

"Man, I'm telling you I don't want to play."

"No, no, no, no. Your turn! You go and do what I said! Your turn to bat."

"Man, I'm telling you, I don't want to play."

"No, no, you're pinch-hitting."

"Man, what's the matter with you?"

Mr. Smirney handed Peewee the bat. Peewee took it and hit Mr. Smirney in the head with it. He then dropped the bat and ran home.

Peewee's grandmother heard the news and phoned his mother at work before Peewee reached home. His mother, through his grandmother, instructed Peewee to stay at home until his father arrived. Peewee would have short-lived hell to pay.

He never learned what happened to Mr. Smirney and he never returned to Wadleigh Junior High School. He was expelled and placed, or sentenced, as he saw it, to James Otis, an all-boys school on 116th Street. Peewee later thought this was why he was never charged for hitting Smirney in the head with the bat. He was already being punished. James Otis was a bad school in a bad neighborhood, the so-called Red Men's district where the gang the Red Men stayed. It was also right in the middle of the Mafia's uptown territory.

10

PEEWEE AND THE WHITE STOCKBROKER

Peter Arrington III sat at his desk in a Wall Street brokerage house and watched a line of late-fall afternoon shadows knife across his office floor. It was December 9, 1962. He had made money for his clients and for himself that day, and he was pleased. Though it was half past four, Peter had scarcely logged half of his workday, which would stretch on long after the market closed.

Beth Morgan, Peter's secretary, stuck her head in the door: "Unless you have something more for me, Mr. Arrington, I'll leave now to drop off those documents."

"No. You go on ahead, Beth. I'll be fine. See you in the morning." Peter smiled faintly without lifting his eyes from the monitor across which the day's closing stock prices streamed. There were two screens in Peter's office. The one he was watching glowed green into the darkening office, giving it an eerie, cold ambience. The other screen was an ordinary television, mounted high on the wall in a corner diagonally across the room from his cluttered desk. The television, as usual, was on with the sound barely audible.

Peter Arrington III was a very forgettable man. He was

thirty-three years old, medium height, medium weight, medium features. He had fair skin and brown-blond, thin hair, which he combed straight back from a medium forehead like the French actor Charles Boyer, whose easy elegance Peter tried, but failed, to affect. Governed by a clutch of insecurities, Peter seemed always to be inclined toward overcompensation of one sort or another. Such tendencies had soured a seven-year marriage and caused him, among other things, to appear, in his choice of clothes, better off than he actually was.

He had grown up in western Pennsylvania in a lower-middle-class, Cape Cod bungalow, leaving it at eighteen to attend a medium state college in the Midwest and, later, a medium business school on the eastern seaboard. Although Peter was always mildly, but nonspecifically, troubled, he was not introspective and, as a consequence, somehow mistook chronic angst for constructive ambition.

His eyes watched the screen with low manic energy as if he were *hearing* from the electronic stock notations the second movement of Grieg's piano concerto.

Peter took painstaking care of all his possessions. His suit jacket could never be found thrown over either of the two chairs that rested in their rug depressions eighteen inches from each other and eighteen inches from the front of his desk. He was an obsessively neat man who allowed one breach of habit: the clutter of his desk. Peter lived to make money. The clutter helped him do it.

He had landed a large new account that day, adding to his growing reputation within the firm for *rainmaking*. A meteorically successful, young black R&B artist had given Peter just after nine that morning an account-opening check for $1 million and asked Peter to recommend stocks for the young artist's securities portfolio. Peter looked down from the screen and picked a particle of lint from his gray, wool, pin-striped, double-pleated pant leg. He had ordered the suit on a business trip to London the summer before from a Savile Row tailor. The suit jacket hung in Peter's closet on a mahogany hanger embossed with the tailor's name above a Union Jack.

Peter stroked the expensive wool of his pant leg and enjoyed a surge strong enough to relieve the angst, if only briefly. He looked at the screen and thought more about what groups of stocks he could recommend to the artist that would produce for Peter the highest commissions. Peter was not only a rainmaker, but an account churner as well. He brought money in, and he churned it—or moved it—from purchase to sale, from sale to purchase. Every transaction (whether called for or not by market conditions) produced a commission for Peter.

Shortly after joining the firm nine years earlier, he had uncharacteristically ruminated about the ethics of making large sums of money moving bits of data to and fro, hither and yon, producing from his end of things—well, essentially nothing. But the odd reflection had passed and Peter had never thought about it again.

He would meet with the rich young artist tomorrow and give him the "treatment" or the "esoterica shower" as Peter liked to call it. It worked on virtually all of his clients, and Peter was thought, by consensus within the firm, to be the firm's most effective salesperson.

Peter always wore his suit jacket when meeting with a client, and he had trained himself to always look directly into the client's eyes when he spoke. He spoke with rock-solid authority, as if there could be no more doubt about the soundness of his investment advice than about the sun's reappearance the morning following. Three-fourths of his spiel would be in a language that could not be called English. To his clients, he spoke trade-speak. He spoke it fluidly and well. It was the language of his heralded "esoterica shower." Faucets adjusted for just the right mix of estimated P/E, appreciation potential, and estimated yield, in order to arrive at the clearest understanding of geometric average by category of rails, industrials, and utilities.

More than anything else in the world, Peter wanted to be rich. He thought about it all the time, so much so that his preoccupation with *arrival* rendered him less efficient than he otherwise might have been at getting there. Dreaming required time and Peter had little to spare.

He began to develop a list of the stocks around which he would develop for the artist his esoterica shower. His mind began to wander. He thought with some asperity about the black singer, *What's he need with all that money?* And then a face he had seen only twice, but not for a year, popped into his mind. A black face. A young black face. *I wonder if the artist knows . . . What was his name?*

Peter's pulse quickened with a stab of fear. Among his many idiosyncratic tendencies was an unrevealed belief in superstition. Why had the face materialized now in his memory? It had to mean something. *This is absurd*, he said to himself. *He was just a colored kid. A hoodlum. There is no way our paths could cross again. No way he could touch me.*

Peter took a deep breath and the memory was gone. He spent an hour reviewing detailed analyses of low-end blue chips that he would mix in his presentation with a recommendation of low-risk municipal bonds. He thought further that it would help to discuss a few no-load mutual fund opportunities. The term *no-load* would render Peter honest and forthcoming inasmuch as he would advise the artist to buy the no-loads directly from a mutual-fund house such as Fidelity Investments because Peter's firm didn't sell no-loads.

At 9:30 P.M. Peter decided to go home. As he moved toward the closet to retrieve his suit jacket and a black, double-breasted, cashmere topcoat, he came within range of a news announcer's voice reading a promo for the ten-o'clock newscast.

"Just over two hours ago, Rudolph Jefferson was arrested at his residence in East Harlem and booked on suspicion of receiving proceeds from the sale of stolen bonds. News-team sources tell us that the bonds in question may be those that mysteriously disappeared from a Wall Street brokerage house a few months ago."

Peter lurched backward in the direction of his desk and nearly fell over one of the guest chairs. He reached the leather swivel desk chair and half-sat, half-fell into it while staring at the television. A black man in his midforties was being led out of an apartment building with his hands manacled behind him. Peter's skin turned wet and cold.

Oh God. Oh God. Jesus. Lord God. Peter's breathing became labored. *Wait a minute. Oh shit. Wait a minute.* He sat in his chair with his eyes closed in an effort to slow himself down, to arrange his thoughts in some sense-making sequence.

Jesus Christ. I knew it. That face I just thought about. I knew it. But who was the guy they arrested?

Peter thought again about becoming rich. The thought that it might never happen, or worse, that he might even be charged with something, or worse still, that he might go—*oh God. Oh God. Shit.*

His thoughts began to race again without pattern or shape

or logic. He consciously tried to think a thought that would make him feel better. For no other particular reason, he thought of the Kennedy family. He'd always wanted to talk and carry himself like John and Robert Kennedy. They were both rich and powerful. But the piece of this thought that provided him greatest comfort was the picture he formed of Joseph P. Kennedy, the father, the patriarch, the builder of the family fortune. Peter greatly admired Joseph P. Kennedy. *There* was a man who did what he *had* to do and turned his family into American royalty.

On the rosewood console behind Peter's desk lay a hardcover copy of *The Sins of the Father* by Ronald Kessler. Peter had read the biography of Joseph Kennedy three times through and leaned upon certain underlined passages as wealth-building scripture.

> *Based upon his grades, Joe Kennedy should not have been admitted to any college, let alone Harvard. . . . The only plausible explanation is that the [Harvard] committee knew he was the son of one of the most influential politicians in the state. . . . As unimpressive as his grades were, they undoubtedly would have been worse, were it not for Joe's practice of slipping bottles of Haig and Haig Pinch Bottle Scotch supplied by his father to his professors. . . .*
>
> *Joe ordered liquor from overseas distillers and supplied it [during prohibition] to organized crime syndicates that picked up the liquor on the shore. Frank Costello would later say that Joe approached him for help in smuggling liquor. . . . Costello was allied with men like Meyer Lansky, Joe Adonis, Louis "Leyske" Buchalter, Abner "Longy" Zwillman, Dutch Schultz, and Charles "Lucky" Luciano. They distributed the liquor, fixed the prices, established quotas, and paid off law enforcement and politicians.*

They enforced their own law with machine guns, usually calling on experts who did bloody hits on contract. . . .

By the mid-1920s, Fortune estimated Joe's wealth at $2 million, equal to $15 million today. Yet since Joe had left Hayden, Stone in 1922, he had no visible job. While he made hundreds of thousands of dollars manipulating the market, only bootlegging on a sizable scale would account for such sudden and fabulous wealth.

Though Peter labored to discern a match, he could make no objective linear comparison of his family's intergenerational trajectory to that of Joseph Kennedy's family. Patrick Kennedy, Joseph Kennedy's father, had grown relatively well off from saloon profits and even more successful in the ruthless state politics of the late nineteenth century. In contrast, Peter's father had been a bland thirty-year county clerk, his mother, an even less memorable ever-aproned housewife. Peter remembered them dross gray as if they were dead, which they were not. Nonetheless Peter had somehow subconsciously submerged the two families in the ethical matrix of a general society that valued little beyond material success. Ethics in Peter's home had been discussed as a term whose only visible surface was academic. Beyond the definitional, the word would operationally mean little to the Arringtons although they gave the entire matter no significant attention one way or the other. Etiquette and manners were more important. They were taught as essential catechisms for standard success.

He must be the rabbit. What'shisname had said that someone would eventually be arrested. Yes. That was in the original plan. He had said so. I remember that clearly now.

Peter relaxed. *Rabbit* was a metaphor he had fashioned from an undistinguished college track-and-field career. He had been a miler. A rabbit was a runner included in the mile field to sacrifice himself to set a brisk pace before dropping out after two laps of a quarter-mile track.

Peter clasped his long fingers behind his head and pushed back in his chair. His basic ponderings had always moved narrowly along a north-south axis. Success/failure. Wealth/poverty. Untroubled by the wildfire complexities of moral nuance, he was incapable of expressing ideas unharnessed by conventions of convenience.

In the words of Kurt Vonnegut's character Kilgore Trout: "Ideas on earth were badges of friendship or enmity. Their content did not matter. Friends agreed with friends, in order to express friendliness. Enemies disagreed with enemies, in order to express enmity."

Like virtually everyone he knew, Peter was not a principled or philosophical animal. But that was not how he saw himself. In fact, innocently enough, he *saw* nothing at all east or west of the crowded up-down axis on which he had carelessly been socialized. He was the unwitting neutralist. Head down, busy in the herd, rumbling mindlessly northward under the inky night's dazzling star of greed, which of course he'd never have perceived as such. He simply was what he was. Largely unknown to himself. Uncontemplative. Wound up. Spring-loaded. Fully programmed. Homed on gold. Decently amoral.

What a nice young man, most any maiden's mother would have said.

His manners are impeccable, most any maiden's father would have added.

Although Peter's parents hadn't been well-to-do, he had never wanted for much. He had owned a late-model convertible in high school. An only child, he had had his own comfortable room throughout the eighteen years he'd spent in the family home. His parents regularly gave him things, but less as expressions of affection than as a balm for the deep, dull bruise of generalized detachment. His parents, however, hadn't been aware of such. For they were much like Peter. In the words of an old Caribbean proverb: *Lizard don't make hummingbird.*

The klaxons of emergency vehicles speeding by on the street below gave Peter a start. The snake of fear stirred in his entrails. He remembered the conversation now well enough. He himself had initiated the contact.

Oh, God.

The black boy (Peewee) had assured Peter that this could never come back to him.

Peewee: "All you have to do is change the bonds from non-negotiable to negotiable. Simple. Then send them blind to this person at this bank. Nothing can be traced back to you. We got a guy to take the fall and he don't know nothing about you."

Peter: "Are you sure?"

Peewee: "Yes, I'm sure."

Peter: "And you've done this before?"

Peewee: "Yes."

Peter: "How many times?"

Peewee: "This be three times. It's easy, man. No sweat. Relax."

Peter: "There will be four hundred thousand dollars in negotiable bonds. I get two hundred thousand dollars, right?"

Peewee: "Yes."

Peter: "I'm still nervous about this."

Peewee: "Look, man, this yo idea. Settle down, we know what we doing."

Peter: "But suppose somebody gets caught."

Peewee: "Somebody *will* get caught. Somebody s'posed to get caught. Being paid to get caught sooner or later."

Peter: "Wh—"

Peewee: "It can't touch you. Nobody knows you but me, and the guy who's gonna get caught don't know me."

Peewee talks into the tape recorder, telling me how it all worked:

"At the age of thirteen, we was beating the stock market. We used to make hundreds of thousands of dollars, and all the things we did was with people in suits and shirts and ties.

"I didn't even know banking until I was grown. I knew back-door banking, you understand what I'm saying? I knew how to beat things. I didn't know how to walk in a bank and say I wanted to fill out a bank account or checking account, but I knew how to beat the bank.

"How? Because we had somebody work in the bank, and it's the same way how we beat the stock market—by having somebody work in the bank, somebody work in the stock market. The only person that ever gets caught is the person whose address all the money went to, all the checks went to.

"The person in the stock market would be connected with the person in the bank. People who had millions of dollars in nonnegotiable bonds, they would change them to negotiable bonds, and we'd sell the bonds, and the money would go through the bank, and the money would always go to whoever's address we said.

"And somebody would tell that person, 'Look here. Now, you going to end up getting somewhere between six months, a year, at the most eighteen months. That's the most they going to give you. But it's going to happen sooner or later.'

"That person's social security number and name became a

target. We was never the people who received the checks. It would just be somebody who we told what's going to happen, and a lot of people, to make hundreds of thousands of dollars, would do eighteen months in a second, in one second.

"We did this for three years. From when I was thirteen to just before I was seventeen.

"The guys on our side got half. The guy in the stock market got half. Nobody in the stock market, in the banks, ever got busted.

"All we were was people who when people wanted to commit white-collar crimes, they need us to do it because they can't do it. They don't want to do it.

"We did this for three different stock-market guys in three different years. And got three guys busted who received the money."

Not unlike Joseph Kennedy, Abraham Goldstein and Peter Arrington cleared their unlawfully arrived-by gains and moved on to better things.

They were white and installed by birth into realms of infinite American possibility. Peewee was black and born into America's bottommost consignment. What *race* had started in slavery, a long-incubated poverty, slavery's parting virus, had all but finished in Peewee's Harlem. He had money. Lots of it. But he could not clean it. He could not make it "respectable."

In any case, Peewee didn't care. He was rich and poor at the same time. He reveled at the top of the bottom. He was idolized by his peers.

11

WEALTH, PRIVILEGE, SOCIAL CLASS, AND RACE

"Before long, my life was like watching a Hollywood movie. Everybody wanted to dress like, walk like, be like, and treat women like Peewee Kirkland. It had gotten out of control. I was driving a Rolls before the movie *Cotton Comes to Harlem*.

"I would pull up at Ruckers [a basketball tournament in Harlem] in a Rolls-Royce after the game. I would charter buses waiting to take people to my mansion on Long Island to party. I wanted people to be able to get out of the ghetto for a little while to get a taste of the good life. I had twenty-six rooms and an elevator that took you from the bedroom to the kitchen. When you've got all this, you need to let people know that life ain't all about poverty. When it was time for an Ali fight, I would buy five hundred tickets at five hundred dollars a pop. Then I would charter planes for the people to ride on, and I'd rent two to three floors in the best hotels. One time there was a fight in Atlanta and we drove down twenty-five cars deep. All the cars were mine. I was the only person in California with exotic car dealerships with every car paid for in cash. Everything was bought with cash. No credit, no loans, all my cash."

"Are you rich now?" I ask Peewee.

"No."

I do not press for an explanation. He has more to tell me first. Purpose looks through his dark, penetrating eyes. He smiles wanly.

He uses the word *I* a lot. *I* this, *I* that. *I. I. I.* But it is not un-attractive. In a lifetime of contest with extreme adversity, the overuse of *I* appears more a warrior mark than a sign of self-absorption. A resilient shell over a soul that, after all, remains likeable.

The privileged receive accolades for the shortest of straight-line journeys. Nicey nicey child with nicey nicey mom and nicey nicey dad in nicey nicey house. Off nicey nicey child goes to nicey nicey college to prepare for nicey nicey career. Oooooooh, everything just as nicey nicey so.

Even when the nicey nicey are naughty naughty, wel-l-l-l . . .

Peewee knows this. It is written on his smile.

While we talk, Mayor Rudolph W. Giuliani, a married man, is a few blocks away declaring that the news media ought be ashamed of themselves for inquiring why New York tax-payers are footing the bill for his girlfriend's security. Perhaps the mayor reasoned that this was all right, inasmuch as Howard Safir, the former New York City police commissioner, had used New York's finest as security at his own daughter's wedding, and later, twelve blues strong, for himself *after* his retirement.

This was just the sort of thing the nicey nicey did.

Peewee knows all this, that such behaviors are tantamount to stealing. But he says nothing, probably believing that stating the obvious is a waste of energy.

It dawns on me that, race notwithstanding, I am, relative to Peewee, one of the nicey, if not nicey nicey. What, when you come right down to it, did I accomplish on my own? A great deal more no doubt than George W. Bush. But, a great deal less than Peewee, who saw but one way out and ultimately found it blocked.

"The drug game is over," Peewee tells me. "The only people making a profit are the real criminals, the ones who create the circumstances, then build prisons to make millions off innocent children who dream of becoming cash-money millionaires . . ."

I think of Governors Rockefeller and Cuomo, the prison industry's yeast brothers.

". . . and wake up inmates trying to make commissary, and that's real."

I think of Frank A. Keating, who is the Republican governor of Rectitude Central, the great state of Oklahoma. I do not know if the middle initial *A* stands for aardvark, a burrowing mammal, but the governor's nicey nicey children have received over the years "gifts" totaling $250,000 from a financier named Jack Dreyfuss. The largesse began in 1990 when the aardvarkian governor was the head *lawyer* at the Department of Housing and Urban Development. Mr. Dreyfuss explains publicly that he gave the money to Governor Keating because Governor Keating helped him promote the use of Dilantin, a mood-altering drug (which is roughly how *Webster's* defines cocaine).

The drug game is over. The only people making a profit are the . . .

The governor who, as I talk to Peewee, hopes to become the nation's top law enforcement officer (attorney general) in the new Bush administration has admitted using Dilantin himself.

. . . real criminals, the ones who create the circumstances, then build the prisons . . .

I look at Peewee. I think: *Just who is really fucked up here anyhow?*

I check my minicassette recorder. It appears to be recording what Peewee is saying. My thoughts stray: *Yes! The piece in the New York Daily News: "President Clinton is on the verge of signing a lease for a suite of offices in Carnegie Hall Tower on West 57th Street, sources said Friday. Clinton, whose lease on 1600 Pennsylvania Avenue in Washington expires Saturday, will take over a full floor near the top of the 60-story high-rise, real estate insiders said . . . at $85 to $90 a square foot the estimated annual rent on the 56th-floor suite that had been home to* Talk *magazine would be $650,000 . . . [the] tab [to fix up the office] could run as high as $200 a square foot."*

Where does he get more than $2 million?

Peewee pushes a copy of *F.E.D.S.* magazine across the table to me. His picture is on the cover. The picture was taken in his criminal heyday. He is bearded and smiling under a large Afro. He wears a white dinner jacket with flaring, satin-edged lapels, a black butterfly bow-tie, and a modestly ruffled, formal white shirt against which hangs on his chest a jeweled necklace with a ruby-and-diamond-studded pendant. Cover language describes the magazine's contents. Toward the top: "Parental Advisory— Finally Every Dimension of the Streets." Across the bottom: "Convicted Hustlers/Street Thugs/Fashion/Sports/Music/ Film/etc.www.fedsmag.com."

I leaf through the pages and come upon Peewee smiling again on page fifty-two under a stingy-brim, white skyff with a layered, white satin hatband. The sport coat is red-and-white checkerboard. Its brilliant color blast is offset by a black handkerchief folded into a triangle pointing two inches above the breast pocket. The black turtleneck shirt is relieved by two two-inch-tall, white block letters arranged one atop the other: *P K.* The hat rests on Peewee's head at a rakish angle. His right hand shakes the hand of a male colleague. His left hand draws back the jacket's side panel and rests on his hip, presenting for appreciation a little finger swathed in gems and a watchband worthy of Fabergé.

On page fifty-four, Peewee, again resplendently turned out, is embraced by one pretty woman while holding the hand of another. His head tilts cool against the angle of his skyff. His scouting eyes look to the left and seem to find still further reason to smile.

I close the magazine. Superimposed on the cover picture of Peewee is this: "Peewee Kirkland: One of New York's Richest Ex–Drug Dealers/Street Ball Legend Speaks Out: Why the Drug Game Is Over."

The title language complicates now my measure of the distance between us. I had thought that I understood him, *it*. I see that I do not. He had not told me about drugs. Out of the blue, I ask a question I had had in my head for years, but had no one to ask it of.

"How does a person just shoot someone dead without thinking about it? Without a moment's thought? Without remorse?"

He appears incredulous, further away than moments before. He looks at me. Again, the wan smile. "You don't understand, do you?"

My innocence mildly unsettles me. "No, I guess I don't. Help me." I am feeling very sophisticated about a square inch of nothing. I try to see myself, but, of course, cannot. If humans could do such, they would bring themselves off differently, wouldn't they?

Unaccountably, the image of Ben Bradlee, the former editor of the *Washington Post*, swims across my vision. Just the night before, I had seen him in a tuxedo on *Larry King Live* reacting to the demonstrators along the Bush inaugural parade route. Some of them, unhappy with the Florida vote tally, had borne placards with the altered lyric "Hail to the Thief." Expending, apparently, much of his talent affecting the bearing of the insufferably pompous, Bradlee plunged full-bore towards the fool's domain the pompous so deservedly dominate: "I wasn't impressed with the demonstrators. They looked a little sloppy." Only when a banality is snorted can it be known to sound truly sappy.

Peewee regards me from worlds away as if I were, God spare me, Ben Bradlee.

"It don't make no difference which way the gun is pointing."

"What?"

"I said that it don't make no difference which way the gun is pointing."

I am at a loss. He senses this.

"Can you expect to value somebody else's life more than you do your own?"

Life. Billions of disparate awarenesses stretched patchwork worldwide on a loom of cold chance. Born under stars. Trapped under rocks. Touched. Abandoned. Taught. Ignored. Starved. Fed. Loved. Loathed. Is this all *life*, or, must any single definition of human *life* be seen, on its face, as absurd? If God exists, had God simply said, "Take a number," after reserving most of the pain and poverty numbers for blacks globally? Was God white and living in Silicon Valley? Was God resting when, on the other side of the world, in the quarter of the wretched, an earthquake swallowed twenty thousand people in India or a tidal wave drowned near as many in Bangladesh? Had God cranked the great natural-disaster wheel of death that seemed to stop unnaturally often on life's black and brown numbers? Had God dispatched Ebola to Uganda? AIDS to Zimbabwe? Or, was God innocent, the suffering man-made? Like the suffering of Peewee's black Harlem in the 1950s.

Whatever *life* was for Peewee in the Harlem of his adolescence, basketball may have saved it for him.

During the commencement exercises taking place upstairs in the auditorium of Charles M. Hughes High School on Twenty-third Street, Peewee shot craps with loaded dice a floor below in the basement. He won almost $400. Peewee had shot craps in the Hughes School basement with better-off fellow students nearly every day of his high school career. He always cheated and he always won. Although he never set foot in the auditorium during the program, he did graduate and he did receive a basketball scholarship to attend Kittrell College, a poor two-year school in rural Henderson, North Carolina.

It got him out of New York. It separated him from Billy Blaze, Blue Juice, and Nervous Sonny. It probably saved his life. Over time, Billy, Juice, and Sonny had become "gangsters." Peewee never saw himself as a gangster. He saw himself rather as an American capitalist, not presumably unlike Marc Rich, the billionaire bond trader who fled the United States for Switzerland in 1983 before being indicted for evading $48 million in U.S. income taxes. Unlike Mr. Rich, Peewee would not have courted business in apartheid South Africa or with the military dictatorship of Nigeria's Sani Abacha. Peewee would have seen such deals as immoral. Nonetheless, before leaving office, President Clinton pardoned Mr. Rich of all crimes and cleared the way for his safe return home to America. The pardon came after Denise Rich, Mr. Rich's former wife, had donated more than $1 million to Democrats, including Hillary Rodham Clinton during her successful U.S. Senate campaign.

Nicey, eh?

The wheels had begun to come off before Peewee left New York for Kittrell. Gangsters hurt people. Gangsters killed people. Gangsters killed gangsters. Peewee was scared. He saw no way out. The *life* was all he knew. It was as if his forehead, all his life, had been lashed to a tree, his eyes an inch from the painful bark that had filled the whole of his sight from birth. With no other frame of reference. No contrast of possibilities. No past. No future. No prospect. No hope. No song of his ancestors' millennial saga. The bark was all he could see. All he had ever seen. Thus, he could not know that his head was against a tree whose leaf-laden boughs opened graceful arms to glorious heavens. He could not see the tree. He could see and feel only the coarse, painful bark. He could not know even that it was bark. Or that it was a tree he was lashed to.

I ask him, "Did you think you were going to die in that life?"

"People was dying all the time, you know what I mean? But once you commit yourself to that life, you're prepared to die, because everything is putting your life on the line, because you have to maintain your reputation, because your reputation is everything. And you don't know when some fool is going to try. I was very protective of my family. People that I knew that liked me could never come to my house where I lived."

"Did your mother and father know what you were doing?"

"My father knew. My mother knew later. By the time I got to Kittrell my mother knew, but my father knew many years earlier."

"What did he say to you?"

"Well, he just said, 'How did it happen?' My father used to gamble. Besides working, he used to gamble. He used to hate Billy Blaze. My father knew. He found out, and he found Billy, and him and Billy had a big conversation. And when I saw Billy, Billy said, 'Man, your father wanted to speak to me. He knew everything.' So I said, 'Why did you tell him?' He said, 'You know what? There's very little I had to tell him.' So when I went home, my father was asking me a lot of questions. And then he said, 'But why? I don't understand it.' And I just told him why. I said, 'Man, because I just wasn't going to put myself in the position. Not that I didn't appreciate the way you and my mother raised us and the way you struggled and what you went through. But I just wasn't going to put myself in a position to live my life that way.' "

The leather lash has little give in it and bites into the back of the head, causing one to choose between the pain of the leather from behind and the coarse tree bark ahead. The pressure of the bark corrugates the forehead, causing pain so intense as to blind completely.

I page through the magazine again. On page fifty-seven, Peewee sits in his criminal heyday on the hood of a large, brown Mercedes convertible. He is dressed to the nines with an open-neck shirt with jeweled ascot under a tan, epauletted Italian-leather jacket draped stylishly across his shoulders. In his right hand, he holds a basketball. He is sitting on bark, wearing bark, holding bark. It is plain from his visage that he does not know it is bark. He only knows at the time of the picture that he is cool. Very, very cool.

According to a 1997 study by the Boston-based Initiative for a Competitive Inner City in association with the PricewaterhouseCoopers accounting firm, African-Americans buy almost thirty percent more clothes than the average American consumer.

Courtland Milloy, columnist for the *Washington Post*, writes: "Even inner-city blacks spend almost 11 percent more on clothing (including expensive shoes for toddlers who will outgrow them within a week) than the average U.S. household. . . . We also spend more than anyone else on electronic products— television sets, VCRs, and CD players—that kill the mind, plus more to fix our hair, which helps hide the atrophy underneath. . . . Add to that the recent reports showing that there are relatively few black honor roll students in most urban public high schools, and you have the makings of a culture of ignorance that thinks it's looking good even as it self-destructs."

On December 22, 2000, fourteen-year-old Herod W. Jackson of Washington, D.C., was robbed of his Avirex jacket and, days later, killed trying to get it back. He was chased down at Martin Luther King Jr. and Malcolm X Avenues in southeast Washington. Milloy writes: "He was stripped of the coat he'd just retrieved, carried into some woods near his high school where he was a freshman, severely beaten, and executed."

We are still *slaves*.

The chains are inside us now. They turn our spirits mean, our hearts into metallic chambers. They strangle the congenital quality of clemency and bind hard the natural life force of positivism. They render our memories empty, our vision short, our song coarse, our fathers broken, our mothers bereaved. They make hopeless our daughters, dead our sons. They shackle our people in differing ways. Some tight by the torso, others loosely at the cranium. They make sightless our leaders.

I, too, am blind.

Peewee dresses these days quite unremarkably. His clothes are no longer statements but just clothes. I refocus in the middle of what he is saying.

"That's what I meant the other day when I was saying when you don't know who you are. You don't even understand what you're saying, because the truth of the matter is, if you understand the struggle that black people went through just *being* black, you understand what I'm saying? Then you'd realize that what I used to be saying was ludicrous."

I look, but I cannot see the destination towards which we are being shepherded en masse like lemmings over a cliff. Heads down, trundling apace hellward, disputing only vigorously the size of pebbles underfoot.

In one black church, the members cheered President Clinton simply for knowing the words to a black hymn.

At a black college, the audience cheered the arrival of the president's seal.

In the first week of his presidency (for which there had been virtually no black support), a black church in Washington, D.C., had given George W. Bush two standing ovations.

Trundling, leaders and flock, heads down intermittently laughing, cheeks inflated, pupils constricted, grousing about the sharp pebbles that carpet the snaking path leading towards the precipice.

"Mr. President, we demand that you sign an executive order outlawing racial profiling."

Is that all they want? Eyes down! Eyes down, I said! Trundling. "Damn these rocks!"

They are all blind. As am I.

I had spoken at Princeton University to a full house: "By the middle of this century, African-Americans, Asian-Americans, Hispanic-Americans, and Native Americans will comprise the new American majority. The United States will no longer be seen, from within or without, as a European-American nation. If we are to cohere and survive as one society, we must take steps now to address the lingering economic, social, and psychological injuries of slavery and the century of legally enshrined racial discrimination which followed it. Leaving notions of moral imperative aside for the moment, it would seem to be in our every practical self-interest to see to it that we fix the long-festering wrongs that have cleaved our nation into warring races and classes. For what is merely morally wrong in 2001, fifty years hence could combust in social disaster and irreversible national disintegration."

I had been lecturing about the themes of my book *The Debt* and endeavoring to demonstrate how reparations for the descendents of American slaves would benefit the whole of our national society. I had described the impediments to social progress largely as pernicious racism and inertia.

Well, before the end of the twenty-first century, history will have proved me naïve. Blind. Well, perhaps not everyone. By the winter of my life, a good many powerful American whites had given a good deal of thought to the changing racial composition of the American population. They had not only thought about it, they had begun to lay a responsive groundwork of plans, prophylactic laws, and public policies well before the end of the twentieth century. They had never met, or at least, if they had, they had never elaborated aloud any theory of racial containment. They hadn't seemed to need to do such. They were Republicans and Democrats, and they enjoyed a kind of useful transparency, as did the laws and public policies they promulgated. While they had likely never heard of him, their muse might have been the ancient philosopher Anacharsis, who likened laws to cobwebs—strong enough to contain the weak and too weak to restrain the strong.

12

WASHINGTON, D.C., IN THE YEAR 2076

Nothing in my great-granddaughter's tenth-grade American history class taken in the year 2076 equipped her to understand the prevailing social predicament of her country or of her people. Her teacher, an Irishman from Chevy Chase, Maryland, named Flanagan, lectured his District of Columbia private school class in the age-old events-and-dates style of pedagogy. There were thirty-six students in the class—one black, three Latinos, five Asians, and twenty-seven whites. The racial makeup of the class accurately represented that of the District as a whole. My great-granddaughter had read somewhere that the District of Columbia's population had at one time towards the end of the twentieth century been predominately black, but she found that hard to believe. Truth be told, she had no idea of what to believe, including why she had to endure Dr. Flanagan, who was a who-where-when robotic bore of a teacher. As far as anyone knew, the word *why* had never passed his lips. But in fairness to all concerned, what Dr. Flanagan taught and how he taught it was not a conscious measure of Dr. Flanagan taken by any of his students, including to a smaller degree, my great-granddaughter.

They were all, well, distracted. Not just the thirty-six students and, indeed, Dr. Flanagan himself, but the vast majority of unincarcerated Americans who lived across the country in gated urban compounds. They seemed to suffer from a malaise-inducing condition described by some social psychologists as information numbness and by others as cognitive distraction. Just how much the laser-powered corporate billboards emblazoned full across the night sky contributed to this emotional disorder was anyone's guess.

In my great-granddaughter's class all but one of the students (a white boy with faux dreadlocks whose nickname was Throwback) had been fitted with mini-transmitter/receivers that had been surgically implanted in each student's ears shortly after his or her thirteenth birthday. The electronic devices, popularly known as The Sound, were all the rage. An implantee could select from a broad menu of stereophonic offerings: music, telephone communication, and instant Internet access, to name a few. Though an increasing percentage of Americans wore the implants (which looked like gaudy interior earrings), the device's manufacturer had enjoyed its greatest success with Americans near the age of my great-granddaughter.

Many attributed this to the availability of limitless music options. But, no doubt, the device's instant-research feature immensely enhanced its appeal to students. (Nearly a century before, askjeeves.com had been the instant-research feature's crude forerunner.)

Little talked about was the government's capacity to make public service and emergency announcements through the device's transmitter and to (and this was even less talked about) *receive* information (billions of bytes simultaneously) from the implantees.

The ear transceiver (as the device was referenced in the product list of its manufacturer) was produced by the New America Electronics Corporation. The company, only twenty-three years old, had enjoyed enormous success under its wunderkind of a leader, Wil Sates, the brash, boyish, strutting storm of haute couture fashion whose flaxen locks, at one time or another, had graced the covers of the country's three major newsmagazines, all of which he owned. Sates, a stratobillionaire, had made his first billion by age twenty-eight. When he was thirty-three, in a speech to a Harvard Business School audience, he had issued the motto with which he would, for the rest of his career, be associated: "Tell the saps what they want and sell it to them." The unincarcerated consumer public loved it. The speech became known to marketing students across the country as the tell-and-sell speech. Americans even turned Sates's motto into a popular tongue twister that went like this: "Tell Sates's saps, sell Sates's saps." Okay. Faster, faster.

In each of the three years running up to 2076, the year that Dr. Flanagan taught my great-granddaughter tenth-grade American history, Wil Sates was named the most admired American by each of his three magazines. By a long shot he was the richest American. His wealth simply could not be calculated, even by him.

On February 26 of the year 2076, Dr. Flanagan's class was silent much of the fifty-minute period. Dr. Flanagan and all of his students, excluding Throwback, were listening inside their separate heads to a Black History Month profile on the life of a late-twentieth-century "artist" named Snoop Doggy Dogg. The profile had been supplied free of charge to American school students by the New America Electronics Corporation, which was thought by the general public to be a first-rate charitable outfit.

At the end of the broadcast, my great-granddaughter raised her hand. Dr. Flanagan ignored her, but my great-granddaughter was nothing if not persistent and continued to wave her hand until Dr. Flanagan grudgingly nodded assent.

"If you don't mind, sir, I'd like to discuss a subject that is more consistent with the spirit of Black History Month."

"Yes," said Dr. Flanagan, drawing out the *s* into a sound that approached a hiss. Dr. Flanagan did not like my great-granddaughter. He thought her at best *inconvenient*, a trendy adjective of opprobrium.

"Can we discuss the national prison industrial complex and its role over the last century in the shaping of American society?" My great-granddaughter had read *this* book. Indeed, the book you are now reading. Decades out of print, she and Throwback were the only students in the class who had ever heard of it.

"I thought it would help us to understand the origins of *the problem*."

Everyone in the class knew of *the problem* from which they were being distracted by the music swirling through their brains, ear to ear. As she finished her comment, a soldier strode past the classroom door. He wore battle fatigues and a heavy metal helmet. On his shoulder rested a loaded semiautomatic combat rifle.

The soldier's presence did not unsettle the students. Instead, it gave them a sense of edgy security. In any case, it was all they had ever known. The soldiers were everywhere: The country had been under a state of emergency since before my great-granddaughter's birth. Crime persisted at epidemic levels. The New America Electronics Corporation and Wil Sates were not unhappy about this. And it seemed that most everyone else was either in prison *and* working there for the New America Electronics Corporation, or living in gated communities with ears (and brains) pierced by the New America Electronic Corporation's wildly popular Ear Transceiver™.

Few recognized how much the country had changed over the years, because there was so little information available about what the country had been like before. For instance, no one could remember when churches had not existed in shopping malls with open fronts and corporate logos just like the stores to which they were joined at the lintel. No one seemed to know either why so many churches were named after Ronald Reagan (The Ronald Reagan Episcopal Church, The Ronald Reagan Methodist Church, Our Lady of Ronald Reagan Catholic Church) or, for that matter, schools, cities, streets, and so on. The Reagan name was everywhere, but no one knew why. In the last quarter of the Information Century, hardly one trivia buff in fifty knew that something calling itself the Ronald Reagan Legacy Project back in the year 2000 had pledged to establish at least one Reagan landmark in each of 3,097 American counties and had launched its drive by building a six-foot-tall portrait of the former president made of fourteen thousand jelly beans, Mr. Reagan's favorite candy. By the year 2010, Mr. Reagan's face had appeared on the ten-dollar bill, and as they say, the rest was history.

The Reagan naming craze, however, had shown signs of slowing after the year 2050. Fresh evidence even suggested that the craze had reversed itself. The reversal was attributed, ironically enough, to Mr. Reagan himself, who had, during his term in office a century before, started successful efforts to privatize virtually everything—schools, airports, parks, streets, airways, water treatment facilities, police departments, prisons, and big chunks of government generally. As a consequence, there was less and less in the public domain to name for Mr. Reagan and, commensurately, more and more to name for Wil Sates, whose New America Electronics Corporation had discovered at the end of the merger rainbow that it literally owned America, lock, stock, and barrel.

Detained in parts of Mr. Sates's lock, stock, and barrel empire were more than 50 million American prisoners, all working for pennies per hour turning out the latest-model Ear Transceiver™, which also projected full-color videos onto the brain. With increasing frequency, unincarcerated Americans could be observed walking about, blank-eyed, watching videos inside their heads.

Everyone seemed to know that something was horribly wrong, but no one knew the *problem's* derivation or how to solve it.

America had become a dangerous place. A Wil Sates company called Freedom Arms, a subsidiary of the New America Electronics Corporation, had sold guns to virtually every American who was not incarcerated and not working for the New America Electronics Corporation or one of its 5,347 subsidiaries.

The soldiers, armed by Mr. Sates and camped on every urban corner, were of little use. Americans were either shooting each other to death with guns made by Mr. Sates or listening to music and watching videos injected into their brains by devices made by prisoners who worked as virtual slaves for Mr. Sates.

Here is what America looked like in the year 2076: thirty-four percent of all Americans were Hispanic; twenty-five percent were African-American; ten percent were Asian; one percent were Native American; thirty percent were white Americans. The United States was no longer a white country. In fact it was seventy percent nonwhite.

Of 400 million Americans, 50 million were living in various

jails and prisons, all of which had been privatized to provide cheap labor to Mr. Sates's sprawling company. Of Mr. Sates's 50 million prisoners, 45 million were black and Hispanic.

Outside of prison, public morals were in an abysmal state. In a boutique display window next to the Westbury Mall Reagan Holiness Church, ganglia of writhing nude bodies could be seen at any given time, even between the midday hours of eleven and one on Sundays. Teenagers strolled past forbearing even to glance, so inured had they become to such scenes.

Throwback started to wave his hand. Dr. Flanagan sighed audibly.

"Yes, Mr. Throwback. What is it?"

"She's right, you know. Instead of talking about the shit we usually talk about in here"—such language was unremarkable—"we ought to be talking about how we got ourselves in this fucking mess. I'm scared to walk to school. I'm scared to be *in* school. Everybody is killing everybody. Poor people killing poor people. Rich killing everybody. Rich people hiding from poor people. Locking every goddamn body up. How is this shit different from slavery, man?" Throwback, who wanted to believe he was black, looked at my great-granddaughter for approval and got nothing. Why should she trust him? No one trusted anyone anymore.

Throwback looked at Dr. Flanagan again. "This country feels like they say apartheid used to feel like in South Africa, man." Throwback's classmates wore vacant faces. This may have been either because none of them had ever heard of apartheid or because they were listening inside their heads to the music that was frying their brains.

A shell exploded in the distance. The classroom's multipanel windows rattled in their frames. Herbert Crouse, a short, fat student who had been slouching in his seat, came upright and croaked something guttural and unintelligible.

"Okay, everyone. Settle down," admonished Dr. Flanagan. The exploding shell had issued a thick report. Dr. Flanagan guessed from the sound that it had struck miles away across the northern line of the city in Maryland, where unicarcerated blacks and Hispanics were concentrated.

Across the country, nearly one-fifth of all blacks and Hispanics were in prison. Of those who were living on the outside, twenty-seven percent were unemployed. Poorly trained blacks, Hispanics, Asians, and whites had become redundant. Most of the jobs performed fifty years before by the poorer classes were either performed by robots or had simply become superfluous.

The national public school system was a pitiable remnant of its old form. Woefully underfunded and symbolized by dilapidated structures, the American public school had become, in all but a few Midwestern and Western states, a preprison holding pen for the country's poor.

The shell, fired by a Maryland National Guard unit at what it later claimed (erroneously) to be the headquarters of an antigovernment cell, landed four blocks from the barbed-wire-topped chain-link fence that surrounded Ronald Reagan Senior High School. When the shell landed, 1,534 students were sitting in classes—807 blacks and 727 Hispanics. No one was injured.

The country was slowly sinking into itself and struggled to disguise a slow nihilistic dissolve with spasms of witty nervous levity.

An uproarious play entitled *Beirut on the Potomac* opened to an all-white audience (critics called it the White House) in Washington, D.C., at Ford's Theater on H Street. The play depicted the three branches of government as three blind mice bumbling witlessly toward oblivion. Harold Snit, the *Washington Herald* theater critic, despite growing public tension arising from what amounted to a national state of siege, called the play "harmless fun." This assessment may have been influenced by Wil Sates, who owned both the *Herald* and the *real* seat of power, which operated quite independently of the politicians, whom he had once publicly referred to as the "jackals under the dome."

Black leaders, however, expressed unalloyed praise for the clueless politicians who appeared to own *them* if not themselves. The Democrats owned their complement of black leaders and Republicans owned theirs. Never had the twain been seen to meet. What pleased the Democrats and Republicans most was that their respective black leaders were the following: famous, trustworthy, and most importantly, completely disconnected from the near half of all blacks who were either in prison or unemployed.

It was not that black politicians were abnormally venal, or even that they were not concerned about the lot of the blacks who had little choice but to live in the war zones outside the fenced and gated residential compounds. Either that, or in prisons, where they were paid a pittance for producing the goods that kept the gated world afloat. It was just that gated blacks, since the passage of the Civil Rights Act more than a century before, had slowly grown apart from poor blacks. They really no longer *knew* them. (They knew well, however, the respective political parties to which their career wagons were inextricably hitched.)

There was at least one other reason why gated blacks no longer closely identified with the plight of their less fortunate brethren. Although members of the white minority continued to see all blacks as, well, *black*, blacks (particularly gated blacks) had since the 2000 census begun to define themselves differently. That census, for the first time, allowed Americans to choose from as many as six racial categories. Blacks chose to be black *and* something else more than twice as often as whites chose to be white and something else.

By the year 2050, there were as many *races* in the black community as there were people: Cablinasians, Hisblanics, Blirish, Blindians, and Blites. It was all quite confusing, which meant that the so-called Brazilian Strategy had worked, at least partially, as its author, Belo Zenith, had predicted it would in the spring of 2010 when his book by the same name had been published. Professor Zenith, a Dartmouth College political scientist of German descent, had reasoned that, with the ineluctable breakdown of the nation state, global financial elites could safely sustain themselves at the pinnacles of material privilege in what he called "the coming ordered disorder" only by denying to the world's wretchedly poor any unifying definition of themselves as a group or groups. Some critical-mass number of the poor had to be given cause to define themselves out economically, socially, and racially so that they would serve, wittingly or unwittingly, the interests of stability and hierarchy—the interests of quiet, and usually anonymous, privilege.

Zenith further reasoned that the poor had to be manipulated with the "opiates of technology" to admire the rich and hate themselves, resulting in the ordered disorder that could be contained and regulated and exploited by a comprehensive private prison system.

Wil Sates was anything but quiet and anonymous. Every

other maxim of Belo Zenith, however, Sates had adhered to religiously. In this spirit, Sates presented a check for $500,000 annually at the NAACP's Image Awards Program. He had gotten the idea to do this upon reading that the NAACP had honored former president William Jefferson Clinton at its 2001 Image Awards program. The 170-year-old civil rights institution had honored the former president for pushing black, brown, and white mothers off the welfare rolls (and into poverty). This impressed Sates, but not nearly so much as President Clinton's courageous exercise of executive discretion that had placed him squarely in the small pantheon of great American prison-building presidents.

My great-granddaughter raised her hand again. Dr. Flanagan nodded resignedly.

"As opposed to being bound to this largely irrelevant textbook, I think we should be discussing the ugly reality in which we are living, and, maybe how we got here."

"How we got *where*?" Dr. Flanagan knew he was being obtuse and was not proud of it.

"You were being sarcastic. But that may be a better question than you think it is."

Dr. Flanagan looked at my great-granddaughter and expelled an audible sigh. In his youth he had thought himself to be a good teacher. But that had been long ago. How could anyone teach under these conditions? He was tired and no longer cared much.

"You *know*, Dr. Flanagan. The war here that nobody acknowledges. The war that isn't a war. The army on one side and the absence of society on the other. Organized guns against everybody else's guns. Privilege against a creedless foe. Bad values against no values. War and death without the possibility of heroism or purpose or victory or defeat or understanding or end. If living is sitting in a lighted room at home, or strolling a street at noon, or driving to school in the mornings, or loving anyone, then I fear to live. Yet, I am afraid to die. For, of all the faces I see, in here, in the streets, in my home, it is death's countenance that I know best. I see it everywhere. In the hollow hostility of those I see outside the gates. In the confusion written on the soldiers' faces. In the despair that marks us all."

She paused.

When she spoke again, she spoke abruptly and more loudly. "Are you afraid, Dr. Flanagan?"

Dr. Flanagan opened his mouth but made no sound.

"I know you are. Everybody in here is afraid. Look at Crouse. We're not just afraid of *them*"—she looked through the window into the distance and felt guilty for having referred to the blacks and Hispanics as *them*—"we are afraid of each other." Then she laughed, a nervous and inappropriate bark. "It's funny that we would be afraid, isn't it, Dr. Flanagan, since we're dead inside already?"

She had thought to stop there, but no one said anything. And then she said, "But you know what, Dr. Flanagan?"

He answered quietly, "What?"

"It is fair in a way. It is the price of privilege."

"What is?"

"Fear."

"Why don't you pursue some research on your question and present it to the class when you are done. How does that sound?"

160

Dr. Flanagan's tone had changed from the day before. He had said this to my great-granddaughter with quiet sincerity before the whole class.

"It sounds fine, Dr. Flanagan." She felt an odd surge of exuberance.

Later, she began downloading articles from the old *Washington Post*, which had decades ago been printed on newsprint. The paper had been bought in 2019 by a Herbert Gathers, two owners before its current owner, Wil Sates. Gathers had taken the paper fully on-line and renamed it the *Washington Herald* shortly after acquiring it. The old-style newsprint had made the paper more accessible to the poor, but Gathers had abandoned the old method of publishing in a cost-slashing measure that instantly increased profits by thirty-four percent.

My great-granddaughter was attempting to plot on a computerized time graph the mood and character of American society over the late twentieth and twenty-first centuries in a way that would explain the sad pass it had come to.

The first article she read had been printed in the *Washington Post* on February 22, 2001:

The President, Topping an A-List Party
By Roxanne Roberts

Talk about a Welcome Wagon. President Bush was guest of honor last night at a dinner in the Georgetown home of Katharine Graham. It was the President's first formal introduction to A-List Washington (actually, let's call it A-List United States) with enough power generated to light up . . . oh, California.

The guests included billionaires Bill Gates, Warren Buffet, and Steve Case; Federal Reserve Chairman Alan

Greenspan, Secretary of State Colin Powell, and Commerce Secretary Don Evans; Henry Kissinger . . .

The evening was officially off the record. Graham, Chairman of the executive committee of the Washington Post Co., declined to release a guest list of the strictly private dinner or any details of the evening, but she commended Bush for his effort to socialize in the nation's capital.

. . . Mayor Anthony Williams was among the 103 invitees . . .

Hmmm, wasn't he the last African-American mayor of Washington? my great-granddaughter thought.

She came upon the mayor's name again in a somewhat less convivial context, recounted in an article printed on March 1, scarcely ten days after Mrs. Graham's private A-list party.

Williams Faces Hostility at D.C. Meeting
Police Whisk Mayor Away After Gathering with
Residents, Angry About D.C. General, Turns Raucous
By Avram Goldstein and Robert E. Pierre

D.C. mayor Anthony A. Williams (Democrat) appealed to angry residents last night to open their minds to his politically perilous plan to curtail services at D.C. General Hospital, but he had to be whisked away by a squad of police and security officers at the end of a raucous meeting.

The security detail prevented more than a dozen angry protesters shouting for the mayor's recall from advancing toward the altar at Union Temple Baptist Church during a community forum on the proposed shutdown of inpatient services at the public hospital.

She thought for a while about what, if anything, the two articles may have presaged. (She also wondered why the church had not been named after Mr. Reagan.) My great-granddaughter then said the word *education*. In a flash, her screen streamed forty-six articles in green print, from which she culled seven, including the following two from the *Post:* the first from the newspaper's February 25, 2001, edition, the second from the March 3 edition:

College Hopes Dim for the Poor
Financial Aid Has Fallen Steeply in Favor of Middle Class
By Albert Crenshaw

. . . In recent years when attention was focused on the middle class, aid programs for the poor have fallen woefully behind. Far from granting free rides to a bachelor's degree, aid programs on average aren't even enough to get a student from a low-income family through two-year community college without a struggle.

In a report released last week, the Advisory Committee on Student Financial Assistance said that federal Pell Grants, the government's principal aid program for low-income college students, cover only 39 percent of the cost of attending a four-year public college, down from 84 percent in the mid-1970s.

. . . Already substantially fewer low-income students enroll and graduate from college than those with higher incomes, and if aid continues to shrink, the gap will likely grow. . . . The report concluded that the primary factor in this gap is economic rather than academic.

Study Finds Racial Bias in Special Ed
By Jay Mathews

Black children are almost three times as likely as white children to be labeled mentally retarded, forcing them into special education classes where progress is slow and trained teachers are in short supply, according to reports released yesterday by the Civil Rights Project at Harvard University.

One of the most troubling findings, researchers said, was that black boys living in wealthier communities with better schools and more white classmates were at greater risk of being labeled mentally retarded and sent to special classes than those attending predominantly black low-income schools.

My great-granddaughter pinched the bridge of her nose and squeezed her eyes shut. She was tired, more emotionally than physically. She gave no thought however to taking happy, a psychotropic drug. Happy was one of hundreds of publicly available euphoria-inducing drugs that the federal government had legalized years before. Ostensibly this action was taken to lower the violent crime rate in the black and Hispanic communities. The real reason (and the effect), however, had been to transfer the remunerative marketing of such drugs from black and brown street entrepreneurs to Wil Sates, the owner of Happy Pharmaceuticals, a company that controlled seventy-six percent of the world's drug market. Sates had first fought hard in the war against illicit drugs and then later, in the successful campaign, to legalize them. He had profited handsomely. The well-to-do could now buy their mood-altering drugs without prescription in a gated Sates Happy Store. Few gated elites could even remember having to shop for their drugs in the black and brown crime-ravaged wilderness beyond the walls as their forebears had been forced to do illegally in the past.

Most of my great-granddaughter's friends took happy in combination with The Sound at high volume. Although the tens of millions who did this were said to appear briefly catatonic, they described the feeling, called happy sound, as a "state of perfect bliss." My great-granddaughter did not like what she had heard about the drug's common side effect, which was an offsetting emotion of profound isolation. For this reason she never took happy, although she often thought that the drug's side effect couldn't be more unpleasant than the standard grayness of a life unblurred by chemicals.

In an effort to anchor her research, she thought of a phrase I had written seventy-five years before. The passage had not been seen as prophetic when it was written in 2001. For those few Americans who had even noticed it, the phrase, in lawyers' language, "assumed facts not in evidence" and could therefore be given no credence at all.

She recited it aloud, which was what she often did to make things seem real:

Americans had slowly and quietly lost their democracy because they hadn't realized soon enough that a vigilance of wrenching self-examination was the price of every democracy's varied privilege.

She understood that America was no longer a democracy, although it still extolled with some bluster the constitutional trappings of democracy. But no one believed it anymore, not even the privileged, who were caged in their gated enclaves as hostages to the comedy of conspicuous success.

She felt isolated even though she had not taken happy, so few gated blacks were there in her compound. As for the blacks in prisons and the rest scratching out existences in the violent netherworlds beyond the walls, she felt a vague ethnohistorical attachment but little else. After all, she had never known one. She also knew, but would never confess, that she was afraid of them. *Them* included all of the poor who lived outside the gates, the overwhelming majority of whom were black and Hispanic. They had been flattened by the gated elites into a single, undifferentiated, featureless, emotionless stereotype that might better have served as a mirror in which the elites could see themselves had they bothered to look. She *had* bothered to look. What she saw confused and troubled her.

Great-grandfather had written that democracy, to remain viable, must be ringed by ramparts of vigilance. What had he meant? Was he referring to government, the general citizenry, or public discourse as a map of public values? Had he meant that every behavior had consequence? Even the smallest?

Using such questions as a yardstick, she began to assemble in her memory more bits and pieces of information from the year 2001. Streaming across her screen as unrelated items, they had meant nothing to her. Taken together, they seemed to suggest the downward social course on which American society had apparently been locked for a long time.

The first such item caused her to laugh when she came across it. An eighty-three-year-old, Democratic U.S. senator from West Virginia named Robert C. Byrd had stated publicly in March 2001 for no apparent reason that "there are white niggers. I've seen a lot of white niggers in my time—I'm going to use that word," a use for which the powerful former member of the Ku Klux Klan had quickly apologized.

Because the character of public discourse had declined markedly since the year 2001, the next item meant even less to her than the foregoing. The man responsible for it was a former professional wrestler named Jesse Ventura, who worked part-time as the governor of Minnesota and part-time as a color commentator for a national television network's coverage of Extreme Football League games. During a game in March 2001 between a team from Los Angeles and a team from New York, the governor of the state of Minnesota said, "Wheeler played that about as good as he possibly could."

In the years before the governor managed to handle two jobs simultaneously, Tip O'Neill, a former Speaker of the U.S. House of Representatives, popped out of a suitcase on a bed in a hotel room peddling on television a corporate product that no one could remember.

Shortly thereafter, Robert Dole, a former U.S. Senate majority leader, showed up in a television commercial as the pitchman for an erectile-dysfunction remedy known to the public as Pfizer's Riser. David Brinkley, for decades a respected television newsman, upon retirement leased his reputation for a large fee to a company called Archer Daniels Midland.

Although my great-granddaughter saw nothing particularly untoward about this, it was becoming clear to her that by the turn of the twenty-first century, practically everyone was willing to do practically anything for money.

It was early April and the days were lengthening. My great-granddaughter savored the short peace between nightfall and "lightrise." Anticipating the assault, she got up from her computer and moved across the room to close the window blinds. Before she could touch the button, the sky was afire in colors of sufficient dimension to dwarf the aurora borealis. The colors shimmered and resolved into the lines of a rakish teal-blue sports car roaring from the edge of the universe into the foresky before turning and streaking off across a black eastern horizon. Then, a still side-view of the car, which favored a supersonic aircraft's fuselage. A disembodied, skywide voice intoned: "From the Sates Automobile Company, we are proud to announce the 2077 Dream, the most advanced motorcar the world has even known."

The Dream, sparkling like a blue diamond, began to revolve slowly on a slender pedestal just as an image of the Lincoln Memorial fell behind it like a curtain across the night. And then the resonant baritone voice familiar to all Americans from television and transceiver commercials boomed: "I have a dream." Behind the wheel of the Dream sat a lifelike computerized image of the twentieth-century civil rights leader, the Reverend Martin Luther King Jr.

She closed the blinds, returned to her computer cubicle, and opened a small drawer from which she drew two small earplugs. She inserted the plugs and tried to recover her line of thought.

King . . . King . . . I ran across something on him . . .

Although she knew the Reverend King had been something more than a corporate pitchman, she wasn't quite sure what it was. No one knew, or at least, no one she knew, knew. This was not strange. Christmas was the republic's most important commercial holiday. Yet, no one knew how Christmas had begun either.

She returned to the *Washington Post* file on which she had earlier located the March 2001 news articles. She said the name Martin Luther King Jr. The characters on the screen floated downward like falling green confetti. Moments later, the characters formed themselves into two letters to the editor of the paper:

I'll let others comment on the merits of the Reverend Martin Luther King Jr.'s famous speech being used for commercial purposes. But I have a question regarding Alcatel Americas spokesman Brad Burns's statement that "with any impactful campaign, you'll always get a handful of negatives." What language is he speaking?

JERRY HYMAN
STERLING

It is an outrage that the Reverend Martin Luther King Jr.'s children have sold his image, and therefore his legacy, for cash. Julian Bond's [chairman of the NAACP] dismissal of the ad by saying that "this is America" is outrageous too. Certain things shouldn't be for sale, and Dr. King's children should be ashamed of themselves for tarnishing the image not only of their father but of a man who served as a leader for many Americans, and for many others throughout the world.

ELLEN WARD
FALLS CHURCH

Her curiosity piqued, my great-granddaughter said the words *twentieth-century civil rights movement*. Stories rolled across the screen entitled "King, Brave New Leader of the Montgomery Bus Boycott"; "King's Letter from a Birmingham Jail"; "President Lyndon Baines Johnson Signs Civil Rights Bill with Reverend Martin Luther King Jr. and Other Rights Leaders in Attendance"; "Reverend King Assassinated in Memphis."

She read each article twice and felt a disturbing kinship to a species of fish that lived in total darkness on the ocean floor without eyes.

She made a mental note to bring the information she had unearthed about the Reverend King to the attention of the members of the Remembrance Club. Comparatively few gated blacks had identified themselves as *black* on the census taken in 2070. Seventy-nine of those who lived in Washington, D.C., were members of the Remembrance Club, whose president, Horace Hightower, a young attorney, worked hard, but increasingly in vain, to keep his members in touch with their history.

She had never heard the real voice of the Reverend King, only the ubiquitous corporate electronic facsimiles of his voice. She said the words *video, Reverend Martin Luther King Jr.*, and finally, *speech*. The picture on the screen was of the National Mall with the Reverend King standing behind a lectern with his back to the Lincoln Memorial. She had seen the same scene in the Alcatel Americas ad that had been the subject of the two letters to the editor of the *Washington Post*. In the ad, the Reverend King had gesticulated to an empty National Mall as if he were not of sound mind. As the grainy, old, black-and-white film of the real 1963 event started to roll, she was shocked to see a crowd that appeared to number in the hundreds of thousands. And then the Reverend King began to speak with a countenance, a certain gravitas, and a timbre different from any facsimile she had seen. It was a short speech, but its message was as fresh to her as her sorrow. Before the speech reached its powerful close, she began to cry quietly. Her back was to the open bedroom door when her father (my grandson) passed by her room. Unsettled by the angle of her shoulders, he stepped into her room to discover her crying.

"What is it, Puddin'?"

He had given to her the nickname I had given long ago to his mother, my youngest daughter, Khalea.

"Oh, Daddy, oh, Daddy," was all she said as her sobbing became audible.

When he saw and heard the monitor, he understood what had happened. He put his hands lightly on her shoulders.

"There is so much and yet so little to say." He had never felt less adequate. "This is not a good time to be alive. Still, they would have each of us die a thousand deaths."

Before beginning her research, she had jotted down a list of questions against which she would apply her energies.

What were race relations like toward the end of the twentieth century? Were there portents discernible enough then that the disaster of the 2070s might have been foreseen? When had greed overtaken virtually all other public values? When had America started to become a siege society? A prison-based industrial state?

The warning signposts she had come upon from the turn of the century must clearly have been ignored by the leaders of that time. She thought she understood why the trouble indicators might not have been seen as correlates of a worsening social condition. What she could not understand however was why they seemed to have been roundly ignored even as forecasters of separate and specific social horrors. What had they been thinking?

On March 30, 2001, the *New York Times* reported, "For the first time in the modern era, non-Hispanic whites are officially a minority in California, amounting to a little less than half the population of the largest state."

Of course national leaders knew even then what this portended for America's future.

Seemingly unrelated to the *New York Times* story were reports released on the same day that corporate stock prices were down across the board for the first quarter of the year 2001. My great-granddaughter noticed, in illogical counterpoint to these reports, that the chief executives of the top two hundred U.S corporations received in the year 2000 sixteen percent increases over the previous year's average, bringing the chief executives' annual compensation to a record *average* of $10.89 million.

She understood how thinkers in the year 2001 could have been without sufficient foresight to envision how the lines of the *New York Times* story on population shifts and reports on corporate avarice could ever converge with mutually exacerbating energy. But they had. Exploding shells, the walls around her enclave, and the Dream ad flickering across her ceiling were evidence enough of that.

It occurred to her to explore what black leaders were doing and thinking about at the turn of the century. Deciding that it would be wise to bracket her request, she said, "Black leadership, January 1990 to April 2001." The screen went blank. Ten seconds later in thick, blockish characters, a typeface distinguishably different from the computer's normal format, this message blinked onto the monitor: "Request cannot be understood." She made the request several more times and received the same answer.

She thought of two black organizations to which she might turn for help. The first was the Black Shepherds Association of America. For forty years, the BS organization had trained officials for most of America's viable black service organizations, including the NAACP. It was well funded, receiving annual program grants from the federal government and the corporate sector, which for all intents and purposes meant Wil Sates. The association's motto was Shepherdship Over Leadership; It Pays Better. The motto had won the National Accuracy in Mottoes Award ten years running.

The second black organization she thought of, the Robert Moses Society, was poorly funded. She was not even sure that its doors were still open. It was named for a great, but little remembered, civil rights leader who had risked his life registering black voters in Mississippi during the 1960s. Later, in 1982, Moses, a teacher of secondary school mathematics, had founded the Algebra Project, which had facilitated the learning of algebra by poor black seventh- and eighth-graders. The objective of the Robert Moses Society was to promote through education and public policy advocacy the genuine advancement of the black community. Moses too had a motto: Leaders Are Not People Who Go Where Everyone Else Is Going. Moses's work may or may not have inspired Chaka Fattah, an idealistic black Democratic congressman from Philadelphia, to introduce in 2001 his Equal Protection School Finance Act to equalize school funding between wealthy and poor American school districts.

My great-granddaughter communicated first with the Black Shepherds Association's computer: "In the late 1980s, what policy position, if any, did black leaders take in response to the beginnings of the prison industrial state?"

She waited five minutes before the answer arrived.

"For what do you require this information?"

She expelled a heavy sigh.

She then made the same request to the computer of the Robert Moses Society. Within minutes, a short biographical profile on Robert Moses appeared on her screen. This was followed by a paper on late-twentieth-century American prison construction presented to the Green Party presidential convention of the year 2000 by Manning Marable, a black professor at Columbia University in New York.

Moses's profile revealed that by the year 2001, the Algebra Project he had founded taught math skills to twenty thousand students in twenty-eight states. It troubled her that while she had heard, of course, of the Robert Moses Society, she had known nothing about who Robert Moses was until now. More important to her than who Robert Moses was, however, was what he had apparently been able to accomplish of lasting value with his life. She thought about the names of black leaders she *did* recognize from the twentieth century, such as the Reverend Jesse Jackson Sr. and Minister Louis Farrakhan, and wondered if these better-known leaders had accomplished as much as Robert Moses, a man she had never heard of, except as an obscure name on an underfunded society. Perhaps she hadn't known of the famous guys' tangible contributions for the same reasons she hadn't known of the Reverend King's. But if, by any objective measure, Robert Moses had done tangibly more than his famous contemporaries, why had history assigned a sunnier berth to them than to him?

She read Professor Marable's presentation to the Green Party convention delegates. She knew a little about the Green Party. Her grandmother Khalea had attended a November 5, 2000, rally for the party's presidential candidate, Ralph Nader, at the old MCI Center in Washington, D.C. Her grandmother, only ten years old at the time, had remembered the rally of twenty thousand so well because I had addressed it, and she and her mother, Hazel, my wife, had joined me, Nader, Danny Glover, the fine actor, and Cornel West, the Harvard professor, onstage at the rally's close. Khalea had related every detail of the event to my great-granddaughter. She had also told her that Nader had been the only presidential candidate to express concern about the proliferation of American prisons and the disproportionate share of our people housed in them at the time. Al Gore, the Democratic candidate, ignored such concerns and still got more than ninety percent of the black vote. For my trouble, big labor, having early on made its deal with Gore, withdrew its longstanding support for my organization, TransAfrica, as punishment for my support for Nader, the only candidate who had unconditionally supported both blacks and labor.

It was with this background that my great-granddaughter read Professor Marable's thoughtful paper. Here are excerpts from what the professor had written:

Along the Color Line, August 2000
Racism, Prisons, and the Future of Black America.
By Manning Marable

There are today over 2 million Americans incarcerated in federal and state prisons and local jails throughout the United States. More than one-half, or one million, are black men and women. The devastating human costs of the mass incarceration of one out of every thirty-five individuals within black America are beyond imagination. While civil rights organizations like the NAACP and black institutions such as churches and mosques have begun to address this widespread crisis of black mass imprisonment, they have frankly not given it the centrality and importance it deserves.

Black leadership throughout this country should place this issue at the forefront of their agendas. And we also need to understand how and why American society reached this

point of constructing a vast prison industrial complex, in order to find strategies to dismantle it.

For a variety of reasons, rates of violent crime, including
murder, rape, and robbery, increased dramatically in the
1960s and 1970s. Much of this increase occurred in urban
areas. By the late 1970s nearly one-half of all Americans were
afraid to walk within a mile of their homes at night, and
ninety percent responded in surveys that the U.S. criminal
justice system was not dealing harshly enough with criminals.
Politicians like Richard M. Nixon, George Wallace, and
Ronald Reagan began to campaign successfully on the theme
of "law and order." The death penalty, which was briefly out-
lawed by the Supreme Court, was reinstated. Local, state, and
federal expenditures for law enforcement rose sharply.

Behind much of anticrime rhetoric was a not-too-subtle
racial dimension, the projection of crude stereotypes about
the link between criminality and black people. Rarely
did these politicians observe that minority and poor people,
not the white middle class, were statistically much more
likely to experience violent crimes of all kinds. The argument was made that law enforcement officers should be
given much greater latitude in suppressing crime, that sentences should be lengthened and made mandatory, and that
prisons should be designed not for the purpose of rehabili-
tation, but punishment.

Consequently, there was a rapid expansion in the person-
nel of the criminal justice system, as well as the construction
of new prisons. What occurred in New York State for exam-
ple was typical of what happened nationally. From 1817 to
1981, New York had opened 33 state prisons. From 1982 to
1999, another 38 state prisons were constructed. The state's
prison population at the time of the Attica prison revolt in
September 1971 was about 12,500. By 1999, there were over
71,000 prisoners in New York State correctional facilities.

In 1974, the number of Americans incarcerated in all state prisons stood at 187,500. By 1991, the number had reached 711,700. Nearly two-thirds of all state prisoners in 1991 had less than a high school education. One-third of all prisoners were unemployed at the time of their arrests. Incarceration rates by the end of the 1980s had soared to unprecedented rates, especially for black Americans. As of December 1989, the total U.S. prison population, including federal institutions, exceeded 1 million for the first time in history, an incarceration rate of the general population of one out of every 250 citizens.

For African-Americans, the rate was over 700 per 100,000, or about seven times more than for whites. About one-half of all prisoners were black. Twenty-three percent of all black males in their twenties were either in jail or prison, on parole, probation, or awaiting trial. The rate of incarceration of black Americans in 1989 had even surpassed that experienced by blacks who still lived under the apartheid regime of South Africa.

By the early 1990s, rates for all types of violent crime began to plummet. But the laws, which sent offenders to prison, were made even more severe. Children were increasingly viewed in courts as adults and subjected to harsher penalties. Laws like California's "three strikes and you're out" eliminated the possibility of parole for repeat offenders. The vast majority of these new prisoners were nonviolent offenders, and many of these were convicted of drug offenses that carried long prison terms. In New York, a state in which African-Americans and Latinos comprise twenty-five percent of the total population, by 1999 they represented eighty-three percent of all state prisoners, and ninety-four percent of all individuals convicted on drug offenses.

The pattern of racial bias in these statistics is confirmed

by the research of the U.S. Commission on Civil Rights, which found that while African-Americans today constitute only fourteen percent of all drug users nationally, they are thirty-five percent of all drug arrests, fifty-five percent of all drug convictions, and seventy-five percent of all prison admissions for drug offenses. Currently, the racial proportions of those under some type of correctional supervision, including parole and probation, are one in fifteen for young white males, one in ten for young Latino males, and one in three for young African-American males. Statistically today, more than eight out of every ten African-American males will be arrested at some point in their lifetime.

She read the last paragraph of Professor Marable's paper a second time, trying to reconcile numbers that could not be reconciled. Next, she read an addendum to the record comprising two items: the first, about Lorton, the only one of the Washington area's five prisons that had remained public; the second, attributed to an organization called the Community Epidemiology Working Group. Although the addendum included no analysis language, she was left to conclude from what she had read that prison system officials must have intended to achieve high rates of recidivism. But why?

Lorton officials knew that keeping prisoners near their families in the Washington area was essential in maintaining the prisoners' emotional health. They knew, as well, the direct correspondence between low inmate mental health and high inmate recidivism. Yet in the 1990s, despite declarations to the contrary, Lorton inmates from Washington-area families were routinely shipped to prisons around the country, prisons that were well beyond their loved ones' ability to visit, some as far away as New Mexico.

During the same period, the Community Epidemiology Working Group reported that American prisons, generally, were so sodden with cocaine and heroin supplies that prisoners were being required to take drug tests before they could be released at the end of their sentence.

She closed her eyes and leaned back in the chair, ruminating.

. . . more than eight of every ten African-American males will be arrested at some point in their lifetime.

She saw in the record no evidence that mainline black leaders in the 1990s were alarmed or even scarcely engaged by the conditions that Professor Marable starkly described, conditions that quite clearly had led to the lawless hell into which she had been born.

The fulcrum years of what had come to be called the Era of Heartlessness ran from 1980 to 2012. During that period, more prisons were built in America than had been built, before or since, in the recorded history of the modern world. After an early collapse in stock valuations in the year 2000, private prisons recovered to provide the economic logic that underpinned the American Neo-Slavery Movement. By the year 2010, America had more than 5 million men and women behind bars. Eighty-seven percent of them were either black or Hispanic. The large majority of them worked in cages for private companies at a wage of less than four dollars a day.

The two men who did most to invest the fulcrum years with philosophical grist were Presidents Ronald Reagan and William Jefferson Clinton.

She knew that blacks in the 1980s had given scant support to President Ronald Reagan.

But could they have misjudged President Clinton so badly? What were their leaders thinking? Had they by then disengaged entirely from the plight of disadvantaged blacks? The poor generally? Had any of them seen what Professor Marable had easily enough seen? Had they known that a third of the families that President Clinton had pushed off the welfare rolls were caused to endure food shortages? That forty percent of them had trouble paying their rent?

My great-granddaughter took out a piece of paper. At the top of it she wrote: *Warning Signs by the Year 2000.* She looked at what she had written and then drew a line through *Warning Signs* and wrote above it *Social Vectors.* She then wrote the following under that heading:

1. Census 2000—projections of a national nonwhite majority
2. Collapse of general stock prices and corporate earnings
3. 16% rise in the salaries of the top 200 corporate executives to $10.89 million per annum
4. Massive nonprison workforce layoffs
5. 375% growth in state prison populations between 1974 and 1991
6. Racial composition of all prisoners—84% nonwhite
7. Privatization of prison labor
8. Apparent indifference of black leadership (curious)

She thought of a story her grandmother Khalea had told her from her grandmother's memory of the year 2001. In the fall of that year, at the age of eleven, Khalea had moved to Saint Kitts with Hazel, her mother, and me, her father. Saint Kitts, a tiny eastern-Caribbean island state, is Hazel's native country. My great-granddaughter knew the island well. During her childhood she had gone there several times to visit her grandmother Khalea, who had returned to Saint Kitts after a distinguished professional career in the United States to live in the house by the sea that had been built by her parents and completed just days before our move there in the fall of 2001.

By the time of our move to Saint Kitts, practically the entire English-speaking Caribbean had endured for at least eight years a troubled relationship with the United States, principally owing to the economic policies of the recently departed Clinton administration. Khalea, seventy years later, could relate the story to my great-granddaughter in such nuanced detail because what President Clinton had done to the democratic English-speaking Caribbean had been a staple of our dinner-table discussions for the eight years that Clinton had pummeled the small, defenseless island states. Khalea had never forgotten it and told her granddaughter as much.

My great-granddaughter turned off her computer and took out a second sheet of paper. At the top of it she wrote: *United States Foreign Policy—Stories Grandma Khalea Told Me from the Year 2001.* Then she began to list the points she could remember:

1. Clinton attempted destruction of banana trade on which islands depended. This done by Clinton to benefit a conservative Republican contributor, Karl Lindner of Chiquita Brands.
2. Caribbean war on drugs undermined by unemployment resulting from loss of banana trade. Clinton policies cause general rise in crime.
3. Countries set up offshore financial services similar to those of the Channel Islands, to provide revenue, among other things, to replace lost banana income. Clinton hostile to these initiatives.
4. Clinton sends hundreds of hardened criminals (born in

Caribbean but reared in America) back to the tiny islands. Weakened democracies cannot absorb them.
5. Apparent indifference of American black leadership
   towards crisis (with the exception of Congresswoman
   Maxine Waters).

She looked up into the ceiling on which an ad still flickered
and thought of two additional points, the first she added to her
foreign policy list, the second to her first list.

6. American markets promised to African nations under the
   African Growth and Opportunity Act disallowed. Former
   Clinton officials say Africans misunderstood the bill's lan-
   guage. April fool.

and

9. Another helpful piece from Census 2000—Washington,
   D.C.'s black population dropped at a sharper rate than it
   had in the previous decade, falling in 10 years from 66%
   to 60%

She placed the two lists side by side and read them through
again. Extrapolating numbers in her head, she could understand now how America had come to have 50 million men and
women in prison, 45 million of whom were black or Hispanic,
virtually all working for Wil Sates.

She wrote down the years 1619, 1865, 2000, and 2076. She
thought of them as benchmark dates through which she could
draw a near-straight line, graphing downward the social course

of American society. She circled 2000 and under it in the center of the page wrote:

What Was Known or Should Have Been Known to Americans at the Beginning of the 21st Century

1. Although it was likely not acknowledged at the time by the overwhelming majority of Americans, the country had by the year 2000 already become a kind of hybrid democratic-police state. This may not make much sense, but this was in fact what America was at the time: a nominal democracy for the upper classes; a nascent police state (de facto at least) for the poorer classes, which were disproportionately black and Hispanic. A new and emerging economic apartheid state. (Note: Whites in the old apartheid South Africa believed their country to be a democracy every bit as much as those Americans who were not wretchedly poor and were outside of prison believed theirs to be a democracy.)

2. Wealth was more concentrated at the top than ever before, in fewer and whiter hands than at any other point in American history since slavery.

3. After the fall of the Soviet Union, the American corporate state, having consolidated its global power via mergers and unfettered globalized operations, exceeded by a considerable measure the power of the declining near nominal democracy that hosted it.

4. America was well along toward putting in place a full-scale prison industrial complex as the answer to its growing race problem and its industrial labor problem. Beginnings of a second slavery.

5. Black leaders said and did little about what their government was doing to blacks at home or abroad.

During the 1990s, an incipient private prison industry had been pioneered by the Corrections Corporation of America. Sodexho Alliance, affiliated with Marriott, was the Corrections Corporation of America's largest investor. Sodexho-Marriott provided food services to some five hundred colleges and universities across the United States.

Upon learning of the relationship between Sodexho-Marriott and the Corrections Corporation of America, students on several campuses launched drives to persuade their institutions to terminate their schools' food services contracts with Sodexho-Marriott. At Oberlin College, some one thousand students and staff took part in a campus-wide protest. In Washington, D.C., not more than half a mile from my great-granddaughter's home, students at American University, seventy-six years ago, had persuaded their school not to renew its contract with Sodexho-Marriott.

From what she could tell, this new student movement attracted little in the way of national attention.

In an unrelated event at the time that attracted broad national media coverage, Timothy Thomas, nineteen and black, was shot in the chest and killed while running from police in Cincinnati, Ohio, on April 7, 2001. He was unarmed and wanted by the police for driving without a license and another misdemeanor or so of like gravity.

She added to her first list the following:

10. Two days of rioting followed the police shooting of a 19-year-old black named Timothy Thomas in Cincin-

nati, Ohio. Shop windows were broken. Drivers were pulled out of cars and beaten. Bricks were thrown into automobiles. Fifteen blacks had been killed by the police in Cincinnati since 1995. Four had been killed within four months of Timothy Thomas's death. What makes the rioting that followed Thomas's death remarkable is that for the first time, as far as I can discover, black rioters had focused their attacks on an upscale, predominantly white neighborhood.

She could now see the present clearly from the past.

A shell exploded and shook her bedroom window. The flash that preceded the shell's dull report washed out the bottom edge of a sky ad that promoted pornographic videos. She heard the wail of distant sirens. *Probably another riot*, she thought, *provoked no doubt by the soldiers.* Gated black leaders would be dispatched to appeal for calm. She'd often wondered why the *soldiers* weren't appealed to for calm *before* they shot some defenseless black child. She'd asked her father once why black leaders were always appealing for calm from wounded blacks whose lives were so markedly different from the lives of the leaders. Her father, with a wry and distant expression, had replied in a curious construction: "Lawd Sates. For Lawd Sates." He'd then chuckled bitterly and walked away.

She felt, in her insight, very much alone. Split off. Sandwiched between blank, coarse walls. There were blacks in prison. There were *free* blacks in relentless poverty across the line. There were gated blacks who had consciously chosen to be anything other than black. Few of the lot of them had any shared definition of themselves or of each other. No shared history. No shared culture. No shared circumstance. Only a common enemy. And even that, they did not share.

They had music. Oh, did they have music. But its thin, sweet voice could not sustain them. For they had little other of a binding memory of their ancient and gloriously successful selves. Thus, each day they were to face, separately and alone, a dawn of paralyzing disadvantage, as if it had materialized fresh and innocent as the morning dew.

She could follow the line of her people's story five thousand years back into time. She was one of a few blacks who could do this in the Washington, D.C., of 2076. Thus, what she leaned upon was not a culture, but a memory of a culture, a culture that could not celebrate itself, even in memory's repose, so long as its contemporary lost children whooped and boogied, grieved and bled.

As ads flickered and washed through the blinds of her darkened room, she thought about the angle and quickened pace of America's social descent. The death of compassion. The normalization of coarseness. The objectification of cruelty. The irrepressible rise of a monotheistic materialism.

Outside the walls, the mornings arrived in ordnance smoke and the stench of human remains. The public parks had long since been closed. The streets were used principally for military cordons. The economy had tethered itself inextricably to prison labor. The national and state judiciaries had reduced themselves to furnace stokers for Engine America. The U.S. Constitution had became a farce to private business.

America had begun the last stage of its social self-destruction. The timbers had rotted beneath its troubled family. No one had come forward who was powerful enough, statesperson enough, visionary enough, to salvage it. The engine had become an an-

chor. The country was sliding slowly downward, its people oblivious, caging, abusing, killing each other willy-nilly en route.

She thought of Wil Sates and the words of Martin
Niemöller:

> *. . . they came first for the Communists, and I didn't speak up because I wasn't a Communist. Then they came for the Jews, and I didn't speak up because I wasn't a Jew. Then they came for the trade unionists, and I didn't speak up because I wasn't a trade unionist. Then they came for the Catholics, and I didn't speak up because I was a Protestant. Then they came for me, and by that time no one was left to speak up.*

Her father was a successful lawyer. Her mother was president of a growing consulting firm. She had an older sister who
was in her second year at Harvard, and a brother in junior high
school, three years younger than she. They lived in a capacious,
well-appointed redbrick home with manicured boxwoods and
flawless lawns.

Her parents loved each other and they loved their children.
That much was clear enough. Nonetheless, they missed something they had never had or never even known had at one time
existed. It was as if they suffered from some atavistic longing
for human engagement that had vanished without flourish
from American social culture generations before.

In the picturesque gated world, all anyone ever saw were
lovely homes and green vistas. In the mornings and evenings,
cars could be seen pulling into chambers with doors that noise-
lessly clamped shut behind them. From time to time, a trophy
dog's genetically altered voice could be heard through a beveled
pane. News that had once been printed on paper and tossed
on lawns now arrived via computer. Currency certificates were
seldom-seen curiosities. Face-to-face commerce had all but

disappeared. Gated people, who befriended only their families and electrons on screens, had separated from each other like oil drops on a still pond.

She had lived in the same house all of her life, yet she knew not a single neighbor—by name or by sight. Society had become a series of concentric circles drawn of thick, unbroken lines. Outermost were the prisoners, separated by a line from the poor, who were fenced off from the gated, who were partitioned by their *things* from each other.

Things were the sole measures of value, the spacers that paced off all separations, physical and social. *Everyone* worshipped *things*. *Things* were like the drugs that tricked their affections and feigned appeasement to their befuddled spirits.

Things were the idols, the gods that pretended nourishment to their moribund souls.

Things, or a yearning for them, were all that joined them, impelled them—the imprisoned, the poor, the rich, the blacks, the whites, the browns—in their dizzying concert of mutual self-destruction. God was dead. God was things.

She could not sleep. She opened her eyes and saw the distorted image flood across her ceiling.

"I have a *Dream*, and now you can have one too."

She put her earplugs in again and squeezed her eyes shut. Eventually she slept.

The sky ads stopped at midnight. Sulfurous yellow light from the street mixed with the green glow from her monitor. Unbidden, a century-old story from a black New York weekly crawled across her screen:

Gangster Ernest Edwards Shot Dead in Harlem.

13

NEW YORK, 1964

I don't *know* that the U.S. government will ever accept its share of responsibility for the 246-year-long *American* crime of slavery and the century of de jure racial discrimination that followed it.

Shortly after this book is published, I will join with a group of distinguished African-Americans in the filing of a class action lawsuit against the U.S. government for reparations on behalf of the contemporary victims, the descendents of American slaves, who have been disproportionately burdened in American society with the social pathologies born peculiarly of generalized abuse and grinding poverty.

It cannot be denied by any reasonable person that contemporary African-Americans have been deleteriously impacted by the social legacies of American slavery and racial discrimination. Yet this simple truth has never been acknowledged by the government that facilitated and benefited from these great human rights wrongs. The victims have never been compensated. They have yet to be apologized to. They have not even been acknowledged as victims. Thus, their damaged condition is rationalized by many to be of their own making. These *many*, who ingest only enough of history to avoid from it any unwelcomed meaning, suffer from a common psychological condition seen in virtually all societies where great human rights wrongs occur. It is called *denial*. Serbs, Turks, Tutsis, Hutus, Russians, Chechens, Germans, the English, the Portuguese, and an endless list of others have been gripped by this responsibility-avoidance at one time or another in their histories. Americans are no different. Yet, they do not usually know it. They are in *denial*. Americans virtually never accept responsibility for any suffering that American policies occasion anywhere. Native Americans destroyed themselves. The North Vietnamese were planning an invasion of New York. Black South Africans actually liked apartheid. On too many occasions like these, the American government placed itself on what came to be seen throughout the world as the wrong side of history, and at a cost of, literally, millions of lives. Perhaps it is because of its power that it has never acknowledged responsibility for anything. Never atoned. Never apologized. Never glanced even at the wreckage left behind.

Racial prejudice is, in part, formed and reinforced from perceptions of unexplained, unattributed behaviors that are not socially desirable. We are all born on a field of universal innocence. Human behavior is learned. But from where?

The child arrives to life with little choice but to dress in the behaviors available. We are all mothered by culture and fathered by experience. These are the molds for all human social development. When culture, our social school, is rendered crippled, and experience, our sensory calculator, registers only unrelenting emotional pain, children have little chance to develop into balanced, well-equipped, and emotionally healthy adults.

The first, immediate, and most important transmitters of social culture and providers of nurture experience are our parents. They cannot give more, however, than they have been given themselves. When the root is damaged, so must be the branch. This was slavery and racial oppression's long-range promise to a contemporary generation of spiritually and economically impoverished African-Americans.

I believe that we will eventually accomplish reparations. But not in time to salvage the most damaged amongst us. This we must do for ourselves. This places a special responsibility upon more fortunate African-Americans (like myself) who were not required from the very beginning of their life to be tough before they could become strong.

It don't make no difference which way the gun is pointing.

No one could recall that Ernest "Blue Juice" Edwards had ever been a child, even though he was only twenty-two years old when he died. Few knew what his Christian and given names were, where he had grown up, where he lived, who his parents had been or where they lived; if they lived at all. He may or may not have slept somewhere on a bed as a child, but he *lived* on the streets.

We people who write and read books have difficulty fathoming such. I have three names. I even had in childhood a nickname or two that never stuck. By a long stretch, however, my most important, most defining, name is, and always was, Robinson. I lived at home with my parents as they had lived with theirs. I spoke proudly the name of my family, my oak. I knew the names of all of its branches. I grew up in the lee of that oak. I believe that I eventually *became* strong. I never had to be tough.

Blue Juice, the man-child, was tough, tough from tender, and doomed probably before he was born. My survival, my flourishment, the full-blown *I* inside me—these happy states are as fortuitous for me as Blue Juice's early demise was for him. He never really had a chance. Not that you would have understood had you known him. Blue Juice was a gangster. Blue Juice killed people.

For 346 years America made official war against its black population. It enslaved. It killed. It raped. It robbed. It deconstructed families. It severed their taproots. It interrupted the intergenerational transmission of values. It demolished memory, culture, society, and self. Some of our families miraculously survived the onslaught. Too many, if not most, did not. Blue Juice, who, because of this, would likely have understood none of this, was one such extreme casualty.

Peewee says, "I loved him and Billy Blaze, loved them thorough, real thorough. But Juice was just dangerous. You could look in his face and see it. He and Billy and Sonny killed people. That's when we separated. I wasn't going to take somebody's life, because it was almost like I always knew that only God had that right, you know what I mean? Not that I didn't think that to protect my family that it wasn't possible, that it could happen, but I knew it was never going to happen concerning money.

"And even when I got in the money-lending game and all them games, I learned to understand that a guy could hit the number and get it, a guy could do something else and get it, the guy could get lucky playing craps and end up with it, but if you took his life, he could never pay you. So, it was senseless to take somebody's life."

Peewee was followed by worlds, one into the next. He would try to close doors, but the doors would never close snug into the jambs.

In the summer of 1964, Peewee returned to Harlem after his first year at Kittrell College in Henderson, North Carolina. Basketball had taken him south to the two-year, church-supported institution and reprieved him briefly from *the life*.

Kittrell was a poor black school in a small country town. I had played there for Norfolk State College against the Kittrell basketball squad two years before Peewee arrived. The gymnasium was a jerry-built, matchbox affair. The score was kept on a blackboard by an attentive student who chalked and erased, chalked and erased. After a rapid exchange of fast-break baskets, the visiting team had little choice but to place its trust in the residual decencies of the rural black South, arguably the last outpost in America unreached by the negative new behaviors that were claiming public etiquette. At the end of game, we looked at the blackboard and accepted the gospel of its numbers.

Peewee had left his long chinchilla coat behind in New York. Still, despite an attempt to dress nondescriptly, he must have stood out from the farm-country student body. Harlem, New York City, was written all over him. By the summer of 1964 he was back at home, out of mufti, and into the flamboyant uniform of *the life*. He was nineteen years old.

He was in the Red Randolph Shalimar bar on 123rd Street and Seventh Avenue at two o'clock in the morning when he heard the news. He was leaning against the bar within earshot of a small group of men who had just entered from the street. He heard one of them say, "Man, they just killed Blue Juice."

It did not register at first. Blue Juice was a five-foot-ten-inch rock of a man whose aura of menace made him seem larger, indestructible even. "The last thing Juice did, he was on crutches at the time, was throw his crutch at one of the guys that was standing over him, shooting him," Peewee says.

Seven men had gunned Blue Juice down on Lenox Avenue near 120th Street. Eighteen months later, the same fate would await Nervous Sonny in his girlfriend's doorway on 127th Street between Lenox and Fifth Avenue.

No one was ever arrested for either killing.

I ask Peewee why they were killed.

"Being in the life. Juice and Sonny had gotten to the point where they had become gangsters. They crossed the line. Like one line is trying to survive and make money, and the other line is when you try to glorify what you're doing and when you just abusing people, and you become a gangster now. You take advantage of other people, weaker people or less stronger people. That's what they went into. Everybody knew it was a matter of time.

"It was so strange, because Sonny and Juice became so well-known in the community, and all of a sudden they both disappeared. I remember coming home from Kittrell and breaking off the relationship when I found out what they was doing and how they was doing it. I remember explaining to them that we had to separate our partnership, that I couldn't be with them anymore. But you know, they admired me for being in college."

Billy Blaze died in a hospital three years ago. He was fifty-five years old. The cause of death was listed as "natural causes." Nobody really knew *what* Billy died of. He was thought to have conquered his drug habit years before.

When Peewee was in prison, Billy started to shoot cocaine. Initially when he and Peewee started "sherlocking" or lending people money, Billy had begun to sniff cocaine. Billy had taken his profits and used them to buy and sell drugs. Then he began to mainline cocaine, shooting it directly into his veins, into his wrists and into his arms just above his elbows.

"It was strange with Billy. I never met his wife, and so I never knew if he really got married, but I met his son. His son, who I talked to a lot about his father, and I could see so much of Billy in him. His son is in the life. He just came home from prison. He just came home about three or four months ago. He was away about three years and he's still in the life. And who knows, I don't know. Maybe it's because Billy exposed him at such a young age that he saw no other life."

An African-American journalist who writes for a large newspaper chain told me that his teenage daughter had been offered an opportunity to go with a high school group to Kenya and had turned it down. When he asked her why, she explained that she "didn't want any spears in my back." The journalist was appalled by his daughter's answer.

As the journalist told me the story, I thought of Mwiza Munthali, TransAfrica Forum's librarian and information specialist. Mwiza came to the United States from Malawi, a country in southern Africa, to attend Iowa State University. For the last sixteen years, he has been my friend and a pillar of our institution. Like others across the continent of Africa, Malawians are social products of extended families (as opposed to our nuclear families). This means that fathers, mothers, grandparents, sisters, brothers, nieces, nephews, and cousins pull together in supporting, rendering service, and providing succor to each other. What little time Mwiza has left to him after he has met his professional responsibilities, he appears to give to his family, unstintingly. To Americans, this should be a compelling (if foreign) notion to observe.

I try to capture Blue Juice, Billy Blaze, Nervous Sonny, the journalist's daughter, and Mwiza in a single frame of sight and I cannot.

It is as if they had been separated by an ageless and powerful foe into tall, smooth-surfaced chambers with greased walls, from which they could neither climb free nor see each other.

Africa's extended-family system of child-rearing died some at home from the debilitating extractions of slavers. It died still more in the Middle Passage, in the plantation canefields of the Caribbean, in the three-and-a-half-century nightmare of the American South. And not a remnant of it could be discerned in the Harlem false childhoods of Blue Juice, Billy Blaze, and Nervous Sonny.

14

FALSE EXITS

When Peewee attended New York City public schools in the fifties and sixties, all of the students in his schools had been black and all of the teachers had been white. The buildings had been dilapidated and ill-equipped. Peewee could not remember being assigned homework. He could only remember playing in school, playing all of the time.

No one ever told him why he was in school. His mother and father had made the nearest thing to an effort, even if they had fallen short. They simply told him they wanted him to go to school. Otherwise, he wouldn't have gone.

His teachers talked, but he paid no particular attention to them. No one else seemed to either. Peewee thought that his teachers certainly knew this. In any case, going on to the next grade had not turned on any measure taken of what he had learned. It had been wholly governed by attendance. If he attended school a certain number of days in a term, he would pass. If he did not, he would not pass. It was as simple as that. Peewee assumed that this was the policy citywide.

Peewee couldn't recall that any of his teachers had spoken of a connection between what was being said in school and what could happen in the world outside. In other words, no teacher in his memory ever suggested that the students were being prepared for any kind of anything. It wasn't that Peewee thought that the teachers didn't care. Maybe some of them did. The problem was that the teachers knew that the students wouldn't have believed them anyway had they started going on and on about the fruits of the education that the students were not receiving.

In any case, Peewee wouldn't have believed them. His parents had tried unconvincingly to have him believe that education could help him survive in life. But he did not believe this, in part because he did not believe that his parents believed this.

"Well, it didn't happen for *them*. You know what I mean? It was just hope. It was what they was hoping would happen. It was what they was praying would happen, but it was a reality that you just didn't see. So I think teachers saw themselves coming to school, teaching, and probably, well, they probably wasn't inspired about promoting, educating, or trying to make young people excel, because they knew it didn't matter no way. Because what was you promoting education for? What was you trying to make young people excel for? The opportunity out there? When it was all said and done, they was never going to get that job that would have paid them that salary to have an impact in their life."

The teachers and the students lived in very different worlds, worlds that were separated by a broad divide, across which passed little that was believable. The *street* was believable. The teachers were not. The teachers said that Columbus had discovered America. The street said that Columbus had not discovered America. The students believed the street.

A teacher told Peewee to study the Constitution of the United States. The street told Peewee that people who looked like him had not been considered people when the Constitution was written. Peewee believed the street and did not study the Constitution.

The teachers believed in America. The students either did not think much about such things or, like Peewee, did not believe in America. They lived in a ghetto. They believed what they saw, broken lives and the unmistakable smell of want.

The students saw things on television, things that they did not have, but wanted. The teachers did not live in Harlem. They lived where the things were. But they never told the students that they too could live where the things were. This was not, as I have said, because they did not want the students to have the things that they had, although some of them may well have felt this way. In Peewee's mind, the teachers simply did not believe that such hopes were realistic.

Peewee drew from all of this several conclusions before he turned thirteen. He was certain that he wanted to have for his family and for himself what the outside American world around him had. He was equally certain that in this pursuit, education was useless. His teachers had tacitly affirmed this to him and to the other students.

Thus, Peewee saw but one path open to him. Had he discussed his choice with his teachers, they would have tried to dissuade him, but without offering an alternative. The street would understand, however, as only the street could. He was only vaguely aware of the nice-sounding homilies that sailed high above his head, homilies that emanated from a variety of orbiting leaders, black and white, near and far, leaders who had the things that everyone appeared to covet but seemed somehow not to want him to have.

Well, what did they know about it? He had friends who were even less fortunate than he, guys who just said "fuck it" and didn't go to school at all, guys who got teased in school because they had to wear the same clothes day in and day out, and then they just wouldn't come, they just stopped coming altogether.

What do the preaches, the teaches, and the leeches know about it anyway?

It was not long after this that Peewee started lending money to people. He told his family about this, but not what he had been doing to make the money in the first place, until, of course, his father confronted him.

"I was giving the money away almost, like different things to people, and it was almost like at fourteen and fifteen, people would come to me with all kinds of different problems, and I'd give them money to solve their problems. And the next thing you know, before I left high school, I was in the sherlocking business and giving money to . . ."

Peewee was lending money to people to finance their connects: $100,000 out, $150,000 back in thirty days. Billy Blaze, Blue Juice, Nervous Sonny, and Peewee had gotten themselves into the credit end of the drug business.

"Look here," a guy would say, "I need to borrow some money. I need to borrow three hundred thousand dollars and my connect . . . to give me my connect, and I'm going to give it back to you in thirty days. I've got to pay my connect so that I can get my product."

And so it went. The four young black men had become entrepreneurs in a grim business. Loans that required no collateral and no paperwork.

"People got to know real fast that we wasn't people to owe money to, because we used to collect money from them. I mean it came to a lot of times sending people to the hospital on the critical list. We was beating people with sticks and blue-steel knifing them too. I couldn't even see them other than the blood."

The largest loan was for $2 million. Cash. To a black guy to pay a connect. Who was a white guy. The connect, higher on the drug chain than the boys' client, was always a white guy.

"It was always Italians and Cubans. It was always Italians at first. See, when Cubans came into the picture, that's when everything changed. With the Italians, you had two Mafias. You had the side of the Mafia that didn't deal in drugs. And you had the side that was renegades, that just didn't care, and those was the ones. The Cubans was just Cubans. They destroyed the game. That's when I got uninvolved, because in the beginning I was involved, but then the Cubans started giving [drugs] to people on consignment. Do you know what that means? With no money. You owe *them* the money. So the guys was dealing with the Cubans; they didn't need me. There wasn't no reason for me to be involved."

15

PEEWEE GOES TO PRISON

When you have succeeded in dehumanizing the Negro; when you have put him down and made it impossible for him to be but as the beasts of the field; when you have extinguished his soul in this world and placed him where the ray of hope is blown out as in the darkness of the damned, are you quite sure that the demon you have roused will not turn and rend you?

> —Abraham Lincoln
> from a speech at Edwardsville, Illinois
> September 11, 1858

Lincoln had been speaking about slavery, in its first American incarnation.

It had been legal. Then it became illegal. Then it became legal again.

In April 2001, an Alabama judge, U. W. Clemon, wrote of overcrowding in a state county jail: "To say the Morgan County jail is overcrowded is an understatement. The sardine-can appearance of its cell units more nearly resemble the holding units of slave ships during the Middle Passage of the eighteenth century than anything in the twenty-first century."

Down the road in the port town of Mobile, Judge Ferrill McRae had been heard telling a young white attorney whose black client had applied for bail reduction that he "shouldn't try too hard because we need more niggers in jail."

Columnist Arianna Huffington had unearthed a place that no one outside of Texas had ever heard of:

"Following an eighteen-month undercover sting operation, 43 residents of Tulia were arrested in an early-morning drug raid. Forty of them were black—an astounding seventeen percent of the town's entire African-American population of 232.

"Almost all were charged with selling small amounts of cocaine—worth less than $200. But as the cases went to trial . . . most without a single black on the jury . . . and the convictions mounted, the sentences looked like something out of the Gulag-era Soviet Union. First-time offenders with no prior convictions—which could have made them eligible for probation—were locked away for more than 20 years. One man with a previous drug conviction was given 435 years in prison; another got 99 years."

On Friday, March 5, 1993, Wayne Robertson, a 230-pound sexual predator, raped Eddie Dillard, his 120-pound cellmate at Corcoran State Prison in California. Mr. Robertson, who was serving a sentence of life without parole for murder, testified that he had sodomized Mr. Dillard "all night long." The next night, Mr. Robertson raped Mr. Dillard again. The incidents received no attention to speak of from authorities, who should not have been surprised by the first rape and should have been prosecuted for complicity in the second.

In Alabama, Cornelius Singleton, a black man who had an IQ of 55 and could not read, was executed for murder in 1992 after signing with an X a confession in which he believed he was admitting to stealing laundry off a neighbor's clothesline. The prosecutor had dictated the confession while Singleton's girlfriend sat on his lap. The prosecutor had allowed her to sit there in exchange for Mr. Singleton's waiver of his constitutional right to silence.

In the fall of 2000, an organization called the Quixote Center looked at legal and police documents from Alabama, California, Florida, Missouri, Virginia, Texas, and Illinois and concluded in a report that, in each of sixteen cases involving a murder conviction, "there exists compelling evidence that the defendant was convicted of a crime he did not in fact commit."

Illinois governor George Ryan declared a moratorium on executions in his state, saying the system was "fraught with error."

Texas governor George W. Bush, seeing no such problem in his state, bore ahead and continued to lead the country in state-sanctioned killing.

No one quarreled with Ken Silverstein, who wrote in the May 7, 2001, issue of *American Prospect:*

"As any student of the death penalty in America knows, the chance that a person charged with a capital crime will live or die depends greatly on race, social class, and—perhaps most important—where the alleged crime was committed. First and foremost is the question of whether a defendant comes to court in one of the thirty-eight states where capital punishment is on the books. If he (or occasionally she) does, the outcome will differ greatly state by state and county by county, depending chiefly on the quality of the local defense bar, the trial judge, and the district attorney, who alone decides whether to seek capital punishment. For all these reasons, the odds are particularly high in Alabama, especially in the port town of

Mobile, and most of all in the courtroom of Judge Ferrill McRae."

It seems a safe surmise that Judge Ferrill McRae, who did not like blacks, ironically enough admired President William Jefferson Clinton, who, even more ironically, was loved by blacks. In his time on the bench, no president had afforded Judge McRae more black fodder than had President Clinton, with whose two terms in office the national incarceration explosion had coincided almost exactly. Indeed, under Clinton, more inmates had been added to prison and jail populations than under any other president in American history. To federal prison rolls, more prisoners were added during the Clinton presidency than during the presidencies of Ronald Reagan and George Bush combined.

In June 1987, towards the end of Edwin Gray's chairmanship of the Federal Home Loan Bank Board, he was summoned to the office of U.S. senator Dennis DeConcini, where the senator and four of his colleagues (Senators John McCain, Alan Cranston, John Glenn, and Donald Riegle) questioned the Bank Board chairman about the appropriateness of the Bank Board's investigation of Charles Keating's Lincoln Savings and Loan. Later referred to as the Keating Five, all five senators had received substantial campaign gifts from Mr. Keating and sought to curtail any examination of his bank's affairs. Subsequently, Mr. Keating was charged with directing the sale of fraudulently marketed junk bonds to tens of thousands of his clients at a cost to taxpayers of more than $2 billion. Mr. Keating had funneled to relatives through his bank's payroll more than $37 million over five years. For crimes described in ninety federal and state counts of fraud, racketeering, and conspiracy, Keating served four and a half years in prison. He is now free and rebuilding his business career.

Michael Milken, a 1968 graduate of the University of California at Berkeley, pioneered the junk-bond network that underpinned the merger mania of the 1980s. Powered by the junk-bond surge, Mr. Milken's salary at Drexel Burnham rose from $25,000 in 1970 to $550 million in 1987. In 1988, Mr. Milken and Drexel Burnham were charged with securities fraud. Drexel Burnham declared bankruptcy in 1990. Mr. Milken served two years in prison and returned to work as the developer of Knowledge Universe, "a cradle-to-grave learning company" that has generated sales of $1.2 billion a year.

In 1983, Marc Rich, the billionaire commodities trader, was indicted on fifty-one counts of tax evasion, racketeering, and violating sanctions against Iran. Before leaving office in January 2001, President Clinton granted a full pardon to Mr. Rich, who had been on the lam in Europe since the investigation that had preceded his indictment had begun.

Not long after President Clinton's pardon of Mr. Rich, Judge Michael Virga, presiding in a Sacramento, California, court, sentenced a thirty-year-old black man named Anthony Lemar Taylor to a term of two hundred years to life in prison. Mr. Taylor had been convicted of stealing $17,000 worth of goods while representing himself to be the golfer Tiger Woods. Among Mr. Taylor's false-credit-card purchases were a seventy-inch TV, a stereo, and a used luxury car.

Prison is hard. The men are hard. The women are hard. The landscape is hard, hard because there *is* no landscape, only prefabricated, soil-gray concrete slabs above, beneath, around you, and bars everywhere, mocking light, replicating themselves in angled shadow like dead soldiers, caging men, women, peeling away all vanity, issuing in their frames and jambs ugly, cold alien noises that freeze the soul and corrupt its primordial song.

Have you been to prison? Did you live there? Did you ever visit someone on Sundays? No? Then you belong to a group that grows smaller by the day.

I went to the city hospital emergency room late one night. Only blacks and hispanics were there. No one said so, but the place was built for us. White people can come, but they seldom have to. Prison is like city hospital. It was built for us. It is just that nobody came out and said so.

Somebody knows something that we don't know. The febrile, dirty lie buried in the cellar of white conscience. The ossified, vertical arrangement of America's colors. The status quo that skulks low beneath the conscious regard.

Michael Milken is back. Big-time. He is back because he was not a "criminal." Indeed, he committed a crime, several in fact, but he was never a "criminal." Peewee, now, was a "criminal." He was a "criminal" before he committed a crime, even before he was born. He was black and poor, ergo he was a "criminal." Whether he was ever actually charged with anything or not.

I too am a "criminal." Reprieved slightly by an urbane manner, but even there, I may be deluding myself.

I may be wrong. I am not white. I cannot know how whites see us. I am only guessing. But, if Peewee is right, *some* blacks in Harlem when he was in the *life* saw him very differently than whites did. And, I mean here, how whites saw the likes of Peewee generally, inasmuch as they were likely disabled by prejudice from really seeing him otherwise. Although it would appear contradictory, prejudice at once distorts, flattens, and objectifies its target behind masks of color, class, and social circumstance. Opinions come premade. Show them a face. Make it black. Put a hat on it. Have it say a few words. Presto. It's a criminal. ID it generally. Shoot it generally. Lock it up generally.

But inside Harlem it was different. At least for some.

"Heroes. Drug dealers are heroes. I was seen as Robin Hood. They're seen as heroes because they are the only people who give something to the community. In other words, all of the problems in the community that the community had, people usually go to the guy through drug dealers, guys who had the money, and they give them money. And they'd help them out, no matter what the problem was."

But guys who are financing the destruction of the community?

"You don't have the luxury of thinking that, because if you need money and I have the money, and you're asking me for it, and I'm willing to give it to you to help you out to make things better, then what are you going to see me as? The solution or the problem?"

But what about the other black Harlem? The stable black Harlem? The Harlem Peewee and the dealers weren't giving money to?

"They saw you as somebody who was a detriment to the community, somebody who was destroying the fabric of the community. I was not aware of this at the time. No, I think I was . . . no, I was more caught up into what the people thought that I was helping than what the people thought that I wasn't. And the reason why is because that's where you play that mental game with yourself, where you tell yourself what you're doing is right, and you're trying to justify what you're doing, because it's . . . either you're too young to understand or too ignorant to face reality.

"And that's what I mean when I said, you know, when you go away, you kind of . . . you don't have nothing but time to think, and you begin to think, and you begin to see how right these people were and how wrong you was. You see what I'm saying?

"And either you know that you have committed your life to a life of crime and really don't care about the welfare of other people in humanity. Period. You know what I mean? So if you're thinking like that, then you go right back to the same thing.

"But if you realize what you're doing and how it's destroying the community, then you don't want to ever go back to that. When I went away the first time, I knew I would never be involved with drugs again."

In 1970, Peewee was convicted in Boston, Massachusetts, of conspiracy to violate the narcotic laws, and sentenced to serve fifteen years in federal prison. The prosecution contended that he had been present during a drug sale that had taken place in a late-model car parked in a Boston neighborhood. Peewee said that he had never been to Boston before being brought to trial there. The jury did not believe him. To this day, Peewee, who admits to committing hundreds of crimes, insists that he did not commit the one for which he was sent to Lewisburg Federal Penitentiary.

They finally had him where *they* wanted him. Don't ask me. I don't know who *they* are. I don't know their *theys* any more than *they* know our *theys*. Clearly enough, seen by each other across the gulf, both *theys* are inscrutable and faceless. The difference is that their *theys* have power, and their *theys* had stowed

Peewee in the rocky ground from which the iron of his cold bars was mined. Here he was, alone with his pride, trying hard to stay a man.

"When I went to maximum security prison, Red Dillon, New York's biggest gangster, said, 'Well, man, you got a lot of heart, and the one thing about you is that we know you'd never flip over.' So they knew I would never tell. I don't know how they knew it, but I guess people in the streets, they can judge character. And they was right. I would rather die first, and I guess they picked up on that."

Peewee was ambitious and smart and elementally decent. He possessed naturally all the suits for American success. But *they* couldn't see him, never *had* seen him, not for a single second of his twenty-six-year life. He was nothing more than an atom in a dense lump, a growing black-brown correctional juggernaut that promised one day to drag down the oblivious sparkling facade of American society.

A judge would later reduce Peewee's sentence to ten years. He would serve four.

By 1981, Peewee would land in Latuna Federal Prison, sentenced to ten years for income tax evasion. Federal authorities would adjudge his income tax remittances incommensurate with his visible net worth. The we-don't-know-what-you-made-but-here-is-what-you-spent rule. The so-called Capone law.

The feds had leverage. They indicted Peewee's mother, whose name was on one of his several trusts. In exchange for his mother's probation, Peewee pleaded guilty. He would not get out of prison until 1988.

In 1990, he would start in New York the School of Skillz and begin to save lives.

New Child Lynch's was one of them.

16

NEW CHILD LYNCH

Wallace Derek Lynch was born on the twenty-first of December, 1975, in Manhattan, New York. He grew up on the east side of Harlem, East Harlem, or as it was also called, Spanish Harlem.

He started life in the Lehman Projects, a high-rise complex on 107th Street. From there, he moved at the age of six, with his mother, Gloria, and older brothers, Aubrey, ten, and Ray, eight, to a co-op named Franklin Plaza. It was a much better place than Lehman. The new building had security and was clean.

Gloria was a housewife. She later went to college and became a social worker. Years before, she and her husband, the three boys' father, had converted to Islam and taken new names. Gloria was about five feet seven inches, brown-skinned, with short, curly hair. Folks said she looked a lot like the singer Patti LaBelle.

Rounding out the family were a half brother, Malik, who was sixteen years older than Wallace and had years before gone to live with his father; a grandmother, who lived in the Johnson

Projects on 112ᵗʰ between Lexington and Third; and a father, who ran a children's clothing store at 116ᵗʰ and Lenox across from the Malcolm Shabazz Mosque.

The father did not move with the family to Franklin Plaza. He had abandoned his wife and three sons when Wallace was three, saying only before leaving, "I'm on a mission." Wallace's mother had said to his father at the time, "Your mission should be to take care of your three sons." But he had left anyway, and although he had talked to Wallace over the years by telephone now and then, he was never seen by anyone in the family again. It is not known now whether he is alive or dead.

Wallace remembers his grandmother giving him baths in the sink of her kitchen in the Johnson Projects. She was a tall, slim woman who told her three grandsons that the family had migrated to New York from Louisiana. She told them how when she was a girl, she had had to walk three miles to school, and how she had picked cotton in the boiling Louisiana sun.

As a grown man, Wallace Lynch would recall of his early childhood: "I remember a lot of love in my house, like my mother talking to us and being there for us. I remember that. The family was tight-knit, at least from what I saw. I remember my grandmother and my mother at that age, you know, I'm saying, when I was really young, seven, eight, nine, ten. I had a great-uncle who lived to be ninety-nine. He lived in New York and I remember going to see him sometimes. But I was real small and I don't remember exactly where he lived."

Wallace said that his father "wasn't a really strong person when it came to people manipulating him and influencing him. And he started messing with marijuana and then she [Gloria] said it got worse."

When the boys were young, Wallace remembered being with his grandmother and how she had helped his mother take care of them. "She would go shopping for herself, food shopping, and would bring her shopping cart full of food to us and things like that."

Wallace had been happy as a little boy. He smiled a lot, so much so that his friends called him Smiley.

But things were becoming more difficult for his mother, who was working, trying to go to school, and bringing up three boys in Harlem all at the same time.

"As I got older, things started to change, you know what I'm saying? We was growing into young men, me and my brothers, and I guess it was starting to kick into her that my father needed to be there. She used to say, 'I'm a woman, and I can't be a man. I can't be your father. I can only be your mother.' And I know it hurt her, because she couldn't. Because we were going through puberty, and we had questions about girls and stuff like that. There was but so much that she could tell us."

Wallace started school at St. Ann's Catholic School in East Harlem on 110th between First Avenue and Second Avenue. He went on from there to the third grade at P.S. 83 and to the fourth grade at another school called Central Park East, or simply CPE. Wallace remembers that his fourth-grade teacher's name was Dottie. This he remembers because at CPE, the teachers were only called by their first names. Dottie was white, as were most of his teachers. She was short and older with platinum white hair. End of memory.

Things went well enough for the boys in the early years. All three demonstrated high scholastic aptitude in their classes. They also developed quickly physically, all showing athletic gifts that were exceptionally evident in Wallace, the youngest. Eventually, Aubrey would reach six feet five inches. Ray would grow to six feet five and Wallace would stop at six feet one, a fair enough height for the special point guard that he would one day become. All of the boys would play basketball and play it well. Wallace, however, would stand apart. The boys did not know if their father had played the sport. They had his genes, but knew little of his history.

According to Wallace, the trouble began when Aubrey started attending Junior High School 45 by the Wagner Projects on 123rd Street between Second and First.

"Aubrey used to come home and tell me certain things about some of the guys in his school, how they were hustling, selling drugs, how they were respected, and as on and so forth. He used to tell me things, and it caught my attention. And growing up, he used to take me to the jams in the park when they used to have little parties and stuff.

"I was always around older guys, older people in general. Whoever Aubrey was around, I was around. Whoever Raymond was around, they were my older brothers and I caught on quick. I wasn't one of those young kids that you wouldn't want to have around, because I was quiet, but at times I was funny. I always had a smile that everybody loved. That's why they called me Smiley. And the other guys loved me. Sometimes the older guys would send me to the store for e-z wider. I didn't know what it was until later. It's bamboo paper you smoke reefer in. They used to send me to the store for it, and I never knew what it was for. And then I used to see them smoking, but I never knew what that was.

"I was coming into my teen years, and my mother was working more, and not being home that much when we came home from school. I know when I came home from school, like I said, everything my brother was doing, I was doing. And it wasn't like he was a bad influence. He was just basically sharing his experience with me.

"And then when I used to be with him, I used to see on my own. I used to see the brothers smoking weed. I used to see the brothers talking to the girls; I used to see the hustlers from around the way that was selling drugs, see them come through in their Jeeps; big gold chains on, and be talking to my brother and things like that."

Naturally, the three boys had quite distinguishable personalities, and this caused them to respond differently to the environment of the streets.

Looking back, Wallace is saying: "Ray was always the straight-and-narrow one. My mom never had a problem with him. Me, even in school, I was always a good student. But I had an attitude. Even to this day, that's something I still work on, my temper and stuff like that. And I pray about it that God will give me strength to just calm it down, and I have a lot, but I just want it to be even better. But like I said, Ray was like the straight-and-narrow one; Aubrey was the one into basketball and the girls; I was the one that just was listening and watching. And like I said, I followed them. You see, Aubrey was more popular than Ray. Ray was quiet and shy. He was an introvert. He was more into himself. He wasn't into everything we were into."

When Wallace was thirteen, he went to live in the Johnson Projects with his grandmother.

"Me and my mother's relationship started to get a little hairy because I would get into arguments in school, stuff like that, and I felt like she was always against me. She would always say it was my fault why I was getting into trouble and this and that. So me and her would get into arguments.

"So I guess she talked to my grandmother and then I talked to my grandmother, and I said, 'All right, I'll ride with you,' just stay with her. And just at least let things clear the air."

And so Wallace moved in with his grandmother and a step-grandfather named Mr. Watts, who was dying of cancer. During this period, Wallace decided to rename himself.

"And I remember I was like, I need a name. What name best describes me? My brother used to call me Mad; my mother used to call me Boo; so I put the two together, Mad Boo, and I said, no, I don't like that. And then I had another one. I don't even remember what that one was. And then I just said, 'New Child.' I didn't like Wallace. I liked Wally. Wally World was the other name I considered."

Shortly after New Child began living with his grandmother, Aubrey joined him in Johnson Projects.

"Mom kicked him out."

Mr. Watts was in his midseventies and had appeared to be in good shape for a man of his age. He told New Child that he had been smoking since he was six or seven years old: weed and cigarettes. At New Child's grandmother's place, Mr. Watts would just sit in front of the television watching baseball with a bottle of beer and six joints rolled up on the table in front of him.

"I knew what he was smoking. I knew he was smoking weed, but he was alway nice to me, even if he was sometimes disrespectful to my grandmother."

The cancer took Mr. Watts very fast.

New Child and Aubrey wanted to be around people nearer to their own age.

"So we would go outside and my grandmother didn't think about it. Where my grandmother lived was a different element of people, because she was in the quote, unquote, 'projects.' So it was more gritty and grimy around there. Brothers was hustling in the projects, in the building, stuff like that. Where my mother lived in Franklin Plaza, there was none of that."

Smart, nice boy, unmoored, starting to lose his way.

"I was going on thirteen when I began really staying with her [grandmother] like that. It just got to the point where, like I said, I was in the street more than in the house. And I seen what the brothers was doing over there. They were smoking their weed; they were selling their drugs, doing their little thing; they wasn't going to school.

"I was into basketball heavy, heavy. I mean brothers seen me when I was younger, every time they saw me I had a basketball, every time they saw me. I used to take one to school. When I was thirteen, I was in Catholic school; I was in St. Teresa. And at the time, I was one of the best thirteen-year-olds in the country. I was an all-American. And everybody around here knew that. I always played with the older guys. I was thirteen playing with brothers twenty, twenty-one, and I was like the only young guy they would even let on the court. But after a while I stayed with the ball, but it was other things that intrigued me, that caught my attention. And that was the money I seen these brothers getting."

No one knew how to contact the boys' father. No one even knew where he was. The boys' grandmother was just that, a grandmother. The boys' mother had lost control of New Child and then Aubrey. It was why she had expelled him from Franklin Plaza. She was at her wit's end.

"It was just when Aubrey, he used to stay out late; that was his thing, staying out late and going to parties. And that was why him and her got into a lot, because he wanted to be in the street a lot and 'do him' basically. That's what we say now. That's the slang now, he wanted to do what he wanted to do, you know, like we say, 'You do you, I do me.' So basically, he wanted to 'do him,' and my mother wasn't trying to hear that. At the time he was seventeen. He didn't get high on reefer; he didn't drink; he wasn't hustling at the time; he was chilling. Actually, he had jobs."

Ray, who remained with his mother, was fifteen and in a private school and doing well. He would eventually attend Bowling Green University and earn a degree in communications. Some innate ability to keep his own counsel may have saved him from the grief of the streets.

"Ray didn't like to party. The only thing that kept us together is the fact that we all used to break-dance together, was called Three Fresh Brothers. But otherwise it was like me and Aubrey, we clicked more, because Ray was just, I don't know, he was just real straight. But I don't think that really separated us or anything. We all got along real well and respected one another, but it was just like me and Aubrey clinged together because we had more in common. We could just talk about more. It wasn't like Ray didn't like girls, but it was just Ray was more into himself and his schoolwork and stuff like that. Me and Aubrey was into the girls. We was into what our peers was into.

"One thing I respect about Ray, at a early age he had his priorities straight. I mean, I can't knock him for that."

New Child was thirteen when he began the ninth grade at St. Teresa's High School. Things had recently gone well for him. He had played on an Amateur Athletic Union team that had won a national basketball championship at a tournament in Indiana. He had been rated one of the best thirteen-year-old players in the country and had won all-America honors. Letters poured in from schools like the University of South Carolina and Syracuse University. In his first season on the St. Teresa's varsity team, New Child averaged ten points and nine assists a game. His tuition at St. Teresa's was being picked up on scholarship.

Half of St. Teresa's student body was black. The other half was largely Latino, Italian, and Albanian. All of the teachers that New Child could recall were white.

"I knew a lot of teachers didn't really care about if I learned or not. I could see that in the way they taught us, because I would sit in class sometimes, and I would see how some teachers would just jot things down on the board. Actually when we came to class, the teacher wouldn't even talk for a minute. They'd have everything written on the board. 'Please be seated,' such and such. Open such and such book to such and such page; read these paragraphs and write down what you think they mean, and they'd be sitting there drinking their coffee and reading whatever they were reading."

After basketball season in the late spring of New Child's freshman year at St. Teresa's, things began to go badly for him. In its hierarchy of officials, St. Teresa's counted a principal, whose name was Brother Raymond, and a dean of discipline, whose name New Child cannot remember with any certainty.

"Brother Raymond was real humble. He was a good guy. But the dean of discipline was a racist. He would say all kinds of things, and he would say it and think it was funny. Somebody would be like, 'I don't really feel like going to class; my stomach.' 'Yes, that's all you black guys say. You all don't want to go to class, because you always want to have an excuse.' He would laugh about it and think that's funny.

"Now we're getting to where things is going to go a little crazy. I got into an argument with the dean of discipline because he choked a young black kid in front of me in the lunchroom. And everybody's sitting there like they don't see what's going on.

"Now, he's got this kid by the neck and he's talking and shaking him and yelling at him. And if you'd seen not only the rage on the dean of discipline's face but also the fear in this kid's face, it just sparked something in me. And I was like no. I can't let that go on. I can't let him choke that kid."

The kid is gangly tall and very skinny. His face is a mask of fright.

New Child yells at the dean of discipline, "What are you doing, man?"

"What?" the dean of discipline answers, puzzled, with his hands still around the boy's neck. "Mind your business."

"No, man. You're a grown man; that's a young boy. What are you doing, first of all with your hands on him and choking him like that?"

"What?" says the dean of discipline, taking a step toward New Child.

"Listen, you come over to me and you put your hands on me, I'm punching you in your face," says New Child, straight, just like that. "You dead wrong for grabbing that kid like that, and I'm not having it. If you grab me like that, I'm punching you in your face or if you even come at me like you're going to grab me like that."

The standoff unfolds in the school lunchroom in front of a hundred or more students. The dean of discipline's Mediterranean complexion mottles in embarrassed anger. He is a squat, strongly built man who routinely inspires fear. Now he is being made the object of ridicule. Laughter ripples across the room.

The dean of discipline walks up to New Child, but instead of addressing him, he snatches New Child's book bag from the lunch table and empties its content of books across the floor. He bellows now at New Child, point-blank, "Get out of the lunchroom."

New Child remembers, "My book bag was on the lunch table. I had my hand on it because I was thinking about hitting him with my book bag if he got too close to me. So, he seen me holding it, and he just snatched it, because it was still laying on the table, but I was still holding it, and he just snatched it and opened it and threw all my books on the floor."

New Child looks straight at the dean of discipline and says, "Do not touch me, because if you touch me, we're going to be fighting." And then, still looking straight at the dean of discipline, New Child laughs.

"Get out of here." The dean of discipline is screaming now. "Get the hell out of the lunchroom. You're out of here. You're finished."

New Child says, "All right." Young-black-male bravado kicking in now. He laughs. Keeps laughing, and walks out of the lunchroom.

Within minutes, he is sitting in a small office across a desk from Brother Raymond, who tells him that the dean of discipline wants New Child expelled from St. Teresa's. And since New Child has been cited once before for chalking a student's back with an eraser, Brother Raymond with his mild manner concurs with the dean of discipline, but agrees to leave the matter in the hands of the varsity basketball coach.

The varsity coach comes down, and while shaking his head the first thing he says to New Child is "I don't know what to do with you." And then to nobody in particular, he says, "I'm not even worried about him; just let him go. He's got a fucked-up attitude."

"And I just looked at him, and I never forget certain things, especially with adults, the way they talk to kids and the way he just had that thing, like, 'To hell with him,' you know what I mean?

"I felt like everybody all of a sudden turned their back on me. I had an eighty-five average in there. I was doing real good. The teachers loved me. I remember I had a global-studies teacher; her name was Ms. Salva. She used to always tell me, like, 'You're very talented in writing. You know how to express yourself verbally,' things like that. And she used to motivate me. She used to sometimes talk to me after class and tell me little things. But they couldn't see that. All they could see was that I was quote, unquote, 'a bad kid.' But I knew I wasn't a bad kid."

It is May. And this was how New Child's freshman year at St. Teresa's High School ended. With expulsion. He is fourteen.

He tells his mother. She tells him it is his fault.

"Then I found myself wanting to escape. I felt like I was trapped. I felt like nobody understood what I was going through because everybody turned their back on me after it; not everybody, but at least the people in the school. I felt they did me wrong. So I went outside and was kicking it with my man and some of the kids from the area, kids I used to play with in the projects. And it was more like they understood more than my own mother and other people, it seemed like. They related, like, 'That's crazy. How they going to do that?' "

New Child is in the streets the next day, still angry about things, feeling dislodged, placeless.

"My man Still Bill from the East Side said that they were going downtown. 'What you all going downtown for?' And they didn't want to tell me at first. My man Benny Light was there and Jesus was there too. Benny Light was not his real name. He was Spanish but real light-skinned, so everybody called him Benny Light. Jesus was Spanish too. He was a Puerto Rican with a slickback. I know there was more people, but I don't remember who else.

"As we walking downtown, they started telling me what we was going downtown for, and that was to rob a parking garage."

It is a warm May Friday, the day after New Child has been expelled from St. Teresa's. They walk at a leisurely pace. Still Bill is the oldest, maybe nineteen. Benny Light and Jesus are seventeen.

"They was telling me what we was going down there for, and I was like, 'What?' I was nervous, but I wasn't like, 'Damn, I need to go back home.' I was like I'm going to go ahead. I went with them.

"I knew one of my mans had a gun. And when we got to the garage, we didn't all go in. We just looked and walked past at first and we was like, 'Yes, we want to get this one.' So, we spread out and stood outside, and my man Jesus went in and just threw the driver in the door. He walked in the booth, cocked the gun back, put it to his neck, and was just like, 'Yo.' If you didn't know Jesus was Puerto Rican, you would think he was a white boy. You would think he was Italian because he walked like he was Italian; he'd fight like he was Italian, but he was Puerto Rican.

"The guy in the booth was Mexican and Jesus puts the gun up and starts pistol-whipping him. He hit him in the head. We run into the garage trying to get the car, because we knew they had the keys in the car. Jesus was in the booth so we figured he could handle the money and we would get the car. Because we was thinking about taking it to the chop shop. So, we run in, and I'm looking for a car. I don't even know how to drive, but I'm trying to get in the car and drive it."

New Child has never done anything like this before. He is not scared, however. A rush of adrenaline has taken care of that. Then Still Bill pulls up in a white, brand-new Honda Civic and tells New Child, "Get in, get in." So New Child gets in.

"While I was running around, I guess Jesus had finished pistol-whipping the dude and left the booth, and he got into a BMW, him and Benny Light. And we just start driving out. They in front of us now.

"In the Honda, we was 'Oh, we got a brand-new car. How much you think we can get for this car, and that?' Still Bill is mad calm. I'm the one that's pumped. I'm the young one. But Still Bill, he's calm. So, I'm more animated and 'yes, yes.' I'm trying to mess with radio. He's like, 'Chill, chill. Just relax.' So, we drive up First Avenue. That was a dumb thing we did, because we went up one avenue for like thirty blocks. We was on Seventy-something . . ."

The two cars are careening through intersections, hitting crossing-street humps, rising off the ground.

"We was going to take the cars back to One Hundred and Twelfth Street and park them there, and then when it got late, take them to the chop shop, we didn't know who owned it. We just knew that the brothers around my block had already taken cars to that shop."

They first hear the sirens as they cross 113th Street. Jesus and Benny Light in the BMW pick up speed. Still Bill floors it and keeps pace in the white Honda with the BMW. New Child looks back and sees the *bo, bo, bo* atop a squad car that is closing on them fast.

"Oh, man."

"Don't look back, don't look back!"

New Child is scared now. He is happy at the same time. This is fun. Now, there is not just the lone wail, but a chorus of sirens accompanied by the scream of burning rubber.

The four, five, maybe six cars howl straight up First Avenue. At 124th Street, the BMW hangs a screeching, oscillating left and opens distance between it and the less powerful Honda, which is struggling to keep up. At Second Avenue, the BMW shoots through the changing light leaving the Honda behind, trapped by moving cross traffic.

In one fluid motion, Still Bill throws the gearshift into park, jumps from the Honda, and runs. He jumps over a gate. He runs across an open grassy lot and onto the sidewalk of a cross street.

"When I turned back around, I was looking at a fat black cop with a Jheri curl. He had a gun to the window and was like, 'Don't make a move. Don't move, don't move. I'll blow your head off.' Because they have a report that we was armed. We already had assaulted the parking lot attendant, and plus there was a lot of us. So, I guess they probably figured that all of us had guns."

New Child has never seen so many police. It seems that six or more hands grab him and throw him from the car onto the pavement. Three guns are trained close on his head. He is saying to the gun barrels, "Yo, I'm only fourteen. I ain't got no gun on me. Why are you all coming on me?"

He is now lying facedown on the street with his arms spread out, cruciform. Hands search him for weapons, money too, maybe. He is picked up off the ground. Now he is able to look around.

"I seen so many detective cars, regular blue-and-white. That's when they had housing police, but they don't have it now. It's just all one. They had the housing cars, the blue-and-white; they had the paddy wagon. I mean there were so many cars out there and so much commotion. All the kids from the projects, they was running out seeing what was going on.

"And they put me in the car, and they was asking me, 'Where's the other car at? Where's the other car?' And I was like, 'I don't know what you're talking about.' I knew where it was at, but they were like, 'Where the other people you was with?' I was like, 'Yo, there wasn't nobody else.'

"All that was going through my head was that I just got kicked out of school and now I was in handcuffs, I was just sitting there in the car. I was like, this can't be. I can't be going through this right now. This can't be real. And then they took me to the precinct. They kept trying to get me to tell on who I was with and all that. And I gave them fake names, fake addresses, fake everything. I wrote a bogus story.

"And the cop, he believed me, because that was one thing I was gifted in . . . writing. So, when he read my story, he told my mother when she got to the precinct, he said, 'I can tell your son is smart, because look at this statement he wrote.' But the statement was just fabricated, because I just lied. Instead of Jesus, I put Pudge. Instead of Benny Light, I put something like Harry. I just flipped everything around and gave them a whole bogus story so that none of my friends would get caught that was with me.

"My moms was hurting. She gave in. I know my moms, she just looked at me. She started crying, and she just sat like . . . she just was crying and crying."

The police catch Still Bill while New Child is sitting in the squad car. He had run into a building and onto the roof, where he hid. The police had no idea where he was until someone in the building told them.

Still Bill will serve eighteen months in prison for his part in the parking garage robbery. Jesus and Benny Light are never caught. The BMW makes it to the chop shop.

As for New Child, "I only did three days. That was my first offense. I was locked up at Spofford in the Bronx. It was late when I got there. And I was like, 'Damn, I'm in jail.' I was just saying, 'I'm in jail.' And I remember, they made us take a shower, and afterwards, they threw some kind of powder on us. It was humiliating because it's like you got people you don't know nothing about standing around you and in front of you, and they just ordering you, 'All right, you got to take off your clothes. Keep your pants stuff over there. All right, turn around.' And you're, like, man. I was just standing there like I can't believe this. I just got kicked out of school, now I'm in jail, now I got to deal with fighting all day, because I used to always hear stories about Spofford.

"Now, see, I don't never want to sound like I don't take responsibility for what I do or what I've done because I do, but I just feel at that time and point in my life somebody could have stepped up and really talked to me the way I needed to be talked to. My mom, she didn't know how to. She honestly didn't know how to deal with me at that point in time. I could tell, because she just basically lashed out at me. She just flipped. My grandmother was more shocked than anything. 'In your mother's honor, how could you go stealing cars? You know that your mom didn't raise you like that, and that's not you.' My grandmother, more than anything, just wanted to know what would make me do that.

"To tell you the truth, at that time, it was just like I didn't care. I was like, man, I just got kicked out of school, and it was like trying to get my mind off of that. That's how it was. It was like, man, I need to get my mind off getting kicked out of school, because I already got beat in the head by my moms about it; she done cursed at me and this and that. I needed just to fly away for a minute. That was like a chance for me to do something to feel good, as strange as it may seem. But I was real angry. I had a lot of anger inside me. I felt like people turned their back on me for no reason."

After expending the greater part of June, New Child's mother won him a place in a regional boarding school. He would be in a new and structured environment—and away from New York. He had accepted the idea and even looked forward to it.

His things were packed and set out near the door of his

mother's place when the phone rang that Sunday morning. His mother answered. She had been smiling. New Child was watching her face when it fell. He had heard her ask, "Why? What happened?" She had listened for a while, and then she had said with incredulity and a measure of anger and question, "You can't accept him? But you *did* accept him. What do you mean you can't accept him?" The voice had turned to frost. But New Child was looking at his mother's face, which had crumbled.

17

WALK-UP RETAIL

In July, Aubrey took New Child with him to his school, Martin Luther King High School, at Sixty-sixth and Amsterdam in Manhattan. "Don't worry about it," Aubrey had said, "you can come there with me." New Child enrolled in summer school and did well.

Aubrey played power forward on the varsity basketball team. Mr. Johnson, the coach, had heard a lot about New Child's basketball skills from Aubrey and had told him on more than one occasion to "tell your brother to come here. Tell him to come to Martin Luther King."

New Child met Mr. Johnson in summer school. In October, New Child came out for the team.

"I went to tryouts in October. I was the skinniest, smallest kid there, and everybody thought it was a joke. I just put the brakes on everybody in the tryouts, because a lot of people had heard about me, but when they saw me play, it was just like everybody was amazed. And I ended up being, when I played for the varsity, the youngest kid on the team. I was fourteen. I was the smallest. And I was averaging twelve or fourteen points and about ten assists as the starting point guard."

New Child was only a sophomore. Aubrey was good, but New Child was better. He was the talk of the school, the skinny kid with the dazzling smile and the moves to match. His future appeared to lie out there, its outlines looming, its sweet rewards shimmering, then resolving. Gift-wrapped, many said.

Towards the middle of his sophomore year, before he turned fifteen, New Child began smoking weed.

"All my friends was doing it, and I don't know, I was just curious. I was real curious. I'd be like, 'Why you all smoke weed?' and they be like, 'Yo, it calms you down.' I used to be like, 'It stinks though.' You can always smell it. I'd be like, 'How can you inhale that?' But after a while you say, 'All right, let me see what this is about.' And I first tried it with my man Manisi in the hallway. His real name was George, but everybody called him Wild Man. I started smoking with him, and I remember I gagged. And I didn't even like it, but the next day I went to the movies with these kids, and they brought probably about five bags of weed and were smoking. And then from then on I was smoking. And then, even when I was playing basketball.

"My mother didn't know and my grandmother didn't know. Aubrey didn't smoke weed, and of course, Ray didn't."

What's more, no one in New Child's family knew that shortly after he had begun that first summer school session at Martin Luther King High School, he had also begun selling drugs.

New Child's crew sold crack along 112th Street most any day in broad daylight. Lookouts were posted at intersections while business was conducted at midblock by boys who were in most cases, like New Child, just barely in their teens. Cheese lines (lines of fifteen to twenty customers) snaked brazenly down the sidewalk to the lookout and around the corner.

Only when a lookout shouted the cop-alert *teddy up, teddy up* would the lines blur and disintegrate, quickly reforming themselves with the all-clear signal. The majority of New Child's customers were white. Many of them were professionals on lunch break from downtown offices. Not a few in the cheese lines were women, some of whom were visibly pregnant.

"Sometimes, we would have more than fifteen people on a line and some would be like, 'Let me get twenty.' Two, four, six, eight, ten, twelve, and you're looking around as you're handing them off and all that, and then they give you sixty dollars; they break out. Somebody else is like, 'Let me get a hundred.'

"We needed some guys out there. Because I'm telling you, the flow was so much that it had to be that many of us out there, because if you had one worker, the worker's going to get swarmed with so many people.

"Some people would come buy two, three packs, so they wouldn't have to come [so often], because some people would have good jobs. You used to see people come up in BMWs and suits and you knew it was probably people that was lawyers and doctors and all had good jobs. And they would come buy your whole stock. You would have five, six packs stashed in your bag, and they would say, 'Let me get five packs.' Sometimes we'd be really thinking they was the cops, but sometimes they'll smoke it right in front of you. Some of the people would come and we would tell them, 'Yo, we think you're a cop.' They'd be like, 'I smoke.' 'All right, smoke one right in front of us. Smoke it.' Yes, they'd pull out a pipe right there. And we'd be like, 'All right, how many do you want?' "

New Child never tried crack himself. Its effect on his customers warned him off.

"Yes, I knew what it was, because you'd see one brother come through one day; he was sharp. Him and his woman would buy some. Three, four months down the line he'd come through. He ain't cutting his hair no more, beard is whipped out; his girl don't look as sexy as she usually do, like she used to, and their car is dirty. Now they want to let us hold their car for a week, two weeks. We'd give them a hundred-dollar pack and ask them, 'How you going to get to work?' 'Don't worry about it.' 'All right.' They gave us the keys.

"We had all races, especially white folk in Harlem. A lot of white people coming down to buy crack. Lined up. Young white people, older white people. It was a lot of black and Hispanic that came, but I think, to tell you the truth, the majority of our money was from white people. They would come and buy five, six, seven, ten packs at three hundred dollars a pack. Professional people. People that have jobs, people who work for the city. That's why I knew crack was not the drug to try, because I said it's making people go crazy."

In part, New Child never sold crack to a cop because, even at fourteen, he knew a crack user when he saw one.

"It's in their eyes. The lust. You can see it. Even some of them that was clean-cut, you could see it. You can see the helplessness, like they just, it's like, I don't know, it's just like you can just tell. Like, I could tell if somebody was a cop. If they came through and said, 'You got some?' 'No, I don't know what you're talking about.' So I never got caught with a direct sale to an undercover, because first of all, I would never sell to nobody that I didn't either see one of my friends sell to, or that they didn't look like they used. They had to look like they used. And like I said, you could tell in their eyes. They just had that look like 'I need to get high.' They had that look like 'I need to get high right now.' "

While there was usually a set price for a bottle or a pack, often the sellers would ask from their buyers whatever they thought the market would bear. Clothes and skin color were tip-offs.

"When you seen people come and you knew they had a lot of money to spend, then I'd tell them, 'No, we don't got tres; we got nickels.' That means we got five-dollar bottles instead of three-dollar bottles. We did this especially to the white ones. We used to get them all the time. Sometimes we'd tell them we got ten-dollar bottles. They'd be like, 'Oh, yes?' They didn't care. I mean these were people with shirts and ties, suits lined up on the street.

"I had bad feelings about some of this at times because when you see how the drugs affect you, especially the women, even at an early age I was just seeing how drugs used to make women sell their body and degrade themselves. And they would do certain things that made me feel bad, but it was momentary. I would think about it, and then I'd snap out of it. It's not my problem, its their problem. They know better. They should know not to mess with this. That was my shield, because I just had to turn cold toward them.

"I knew guys whose mothers would start selling themselves to get the crack. It made me feel bad because it was like you would see the guys, you would kick it with them, probably smoke some weed with them, and then later on their mom's coming up to you saying, 'You got the works?' 'Yes.' 'Let me get five.' "

New Child usually worked his sales post with four guys, all whacked out of their heads on weed. He was angry and lost and unimpressed at the time by lectures about black self-destruction.

"It's sad because my mother did try to teach me about my history and about my family, but it's like when I was doing that, the weed and the selling and all, I didn't really care. It didn't matter to me. The only time it hit me hard was when I seen pregnant women come, some eight months pregnant, about to drop, and I remember I wouldn't sell it to them at one point; like when they tried, I was like, 'Hell, no, I'm not selling you no drugs.' I was like, 'No, because that's a baby in-side her, and that baby don't have no choice.' Some of my friends would be like, 'All right, you won't? How many do you want?' And sometimes they would come and get ten, fifteen bottles."

The people that New Child and his friends worked for bought the crack they sold on 112ᵗʰ Street from the Domini-cans. They would go uptown and buy it wholesale.

"The Dominicans had all the coke and they still do. They were black Dominicans with Jheri curls and all that. Some of them don't speak a lick of English, but they know how to count the money."

The product would then be brought to a Harlem stash house, cut up, and placed in color-coded plastic bottles, ready for sale to customers on the cheese lines. New Child's crew was called the Lynch Mob. The Lynch Mob's plastic crack bottles always bore, like a corporate logo, a black plastic cap.

"You put on a certain colored top so that when people come to buy, they know it's your product. So, when I first started, I was going to use a black top so they knew who had that black top. My group was called the Lynch Mob, at least for a minute. But I didn't really rock with them too much, because I didn't really like them. They were too jealous, and that jealousy would later come back on my family."

New Child was fourteen and making well more than $1,000 a week. "Tell you the truth, I wasn't even thinking about no job, because it was summer youth. That was the only job I could get as far as I saw it. And I was like, 'No.' Back then I think they was paying like three seventy-five an hour, something like that, and that was '89. So, when I seen how much money my friends was getting . . . You could make over a thousand a week selling crack, let alone the brothers we was working for. They was making about fifteen thousand dollars a week."

The standard economic rules of mainstream free enterprise appeared to apply to crack merchandising in many ways. The crack was marketed in different-sized bottles. Some were 031s. Some were 022s. Some were long. Some were short. The people New Child worked for undercut their competition by packing the big bottles and selling them for three dollars, well under the going rate for so large a bottle. The result was greater overall revenues for the retailers, higher commissions for the salesmen, and cheese lines around the block.

"I used to get more than a thousand dollars a week, because you figure in a day's time, plus they starting bottling it up. So, when I used to bottle it up, I knew they wasn't paying me what I was supposed to get, so I stashed some. So, I would have some of the brothers that we had working for us, I would sell what they told me to sell a month, and I would make my money off of that, plus I would stash like six, seven packs [at one hundred bottles a pack]. So, they was only giving us a quarter off a three-dollar bottle, right? Or fifty cents off a three-dollar bottle. So we were maybe getting like twenty-five dollars a pack. Now it seemed like no money, but it was going so fast that before you knew it, you was leaving there with about four hundred dollars in your pocket at the end of the night. But I was doing my own thing, so I was getting more money that was substantial. At one time, I had close to ten thousand dollars over at my grandmother's house. I had just turned fifteen."

New Child was not flashy with his money. He spent money on food for his grandmother's house, a little on a movie for him and a girlfriend now and then, and a reasonable amount on weed to get high. The rest he saved assiduously.

"I used to always stash my money, put my money away, put my money away, put my money away."

Literally hundreds of people saw New Child at midday selling crack on the street in front of the projects. Thus, it came as no surprise to him when neighbors told his grandmother just what kind of work her grandson had been doing for well on to a year.

"They would tell my grandmother. They wouldn't tell me, but they'd tell her. And she'd tell me like, 'Yes, Mrs. So-and-So said she saw you out there. You had a crowd of people around you, and you were selling drugs.' But my grandmother knew what I was doing. She knew what I was doing."

Of course Aubrey had always known. While he had never sold crack on the street, he, from time to time, had chipped in to help cut up and bottle the crack in the stash house. Aubrey was seen to dabble. Nobody thought his role qualified him as a "hustler."

Because New Child's spending habits and taste in clothes were minimalist, his mother and his brother Ray might never have learned of his hustling had his grandmother not told them. His mother had said to him sadly, "I would have never knew you were selling drugs if I didn't see you."

18

AUBREY LYNCH

Author: *Why is it, do you think, that you never thought about the broader consequences to the black community of what you were doing?*

New Child: *It's sad but us young brothers, it's like we don't . . . nobody takes time to really let us know what a community is really about, how we was talking earlier, how we supposed to look out for one another, how we supposed to respect one another, and talk to each other and things like that. And if we really love one another, there's certain things we will do for each other and with each other and things that we won't.*

Author: *Did you ever have a teacher or coach or anybody to play that role in your early life?*

New Child: *Nobody.*

Author: *Did anybody ever tell you that you could be a doctor or a lawyer or a teacher?*

New Child: *My brother Aubrey used to tell me that. He used to tell me, "You're smart, you can do a lot with your life," things of that nature, even when I was selling drugs.*

—From an interview conducted in
New York on April 28, 2000

There is space in the summer night, even in the city's menacing interior. The space is topless. It is open and private all at once, affording city dwellers a fickle security in which they seem, for the moment, their mothers' carefree children again. The summer night draws them, like some compelling primal attraction, out of the anonymous buildings and onto stoops and steps. The young and the old, their voices carrying in the warm night air. Grandmothers laughing. Men boasting. Boys rhyming. Tales told. Stories embellished. Songs crooned. The ageless summer memories that endure.

Tonight is such a night. It is a breezy, warm August 30 evening in 1991. Some thirty teenagers stand, sit, lean, in the public areas in front of the Franklin Plaza apartments on 107th Street and Third Avenue. It is shortly after 10:00 P.M. The young people are broken up into several groups with several discussions going at the same time. Most of the talk focuses on the past and the future, what they did last night, and what they might still decide to do later tonight. The three Lynch brothers, Aubrey, Ray, and New Child, are here. They are standing together, talking in a group of seven, midway on the sidewalk in front of their mother's building. Aubrey is talking as his brothers and the others listen nearby. He cannot be heard beyond his immediate circle, but at six feet five inches and 240 pounds, he can be seen from a good distance, as can his two taller-than-average brothers. Aubrey has a likeable personality and is naturally entertaining. Ray, seventeen, remains the quietly studious brother, bound soon for college. New Child, fifteen, is a mix of identities: rebel, hustler, athlete, loyalist, writer, rhymer, avenger, insightful soul. Child still. Whole man coming.

A few minutes before eleven, New Child and ten friends decide to catch a late movie. Their departure precipitates a breakup of the larger gathering, which, by midnight, shrinks to twelve. Aubrey and Ray, standing next to each other, remain on the street in front of Franklin Plaza talking with friends.

A short, white Puerto Rican boy and a somewhat taller African-American boy, both appearing to be about seventeen, walk along the sidewalk and stop on the edge of the group. The Puerto Rican boy starts to stare at Aubrey. Aubrey ignores him. The Puerto Rican remains still, a few feet off the group, and continues to stare.

One of the twelve in the group asks Aubrey, "Why is he looking at you like that?"

"I don't know," Aubrey answers. But Aubrey *does* know. The Puerto Rican's name is Julio. Aubrey does not know him, but has heard that some while back, a childhood friend of his had shot Julio in the mouth. The African-American boy, Aubrey does not recognize at all.

Julio's stare parts the group. Ray stands fast next to his brother. Aubrey, for the first time, looks directly at Julio.

Julio says, "What you looking at?"

Aubrey says, "What you talking about? You looking at me; I'm looking at you. Ain't no problem. We just looking at each other."

Julio says, "Fuck you, motherfucka. Fuck you."

Aubrey says, "Listen, I ain't got no problem with you; I don't have no beef with you. Go ahead. You're too little for me. I'm not even trying to get into nothing with you."

Julio pauses and looks to his right at his man, the African-American boy, who has not said a word. Julio says to him, "Pass me the joint." The African-American boy pulls a gun from a pocket in his blousy jacket. But, instead of handing it to

Julio, he raises it in one motion and shoots Aubrey in the face, point-blank.

Julio and the African-American boy run. Aubrey is lying on his side with an eyeball dislodged and resting near his cheek on the sidewalk like a wet marble.

Ray chases the two boys, but then catches himself and returns to Aubrey's side. Aubrey struggles to talk, but all he can manage is, "Ray . . ."

Ray says into Aubrey's ear, "Don't try to talk, just . . . I know you're going to be all right. We are going to get an ambulance for you."

Aubrey is bleeding badly. Ray does not know how to stanch the flow of blood. An ambulance has been called. Five, now ten minutes, pass. Aubrey is still alive. No ambulance.

Finally, Ray hears the warble of the siren. The ambulance slows and pulls near enough to the sidewalk for driver and attendant to see Aubrey bleeding on the pavement. Two of Aubrey and Ray's friends move toward the ambulance to direct its approach. Within seconds, the ambulance driver veers away from the curb and accelerates, leaving Aubrey, still alive but bleeding profusely, on the ground.

A second call is made. Ray is speaking into Aubrey's ear, "Hold on, Aubrey. Hold on. We are going to get you to the hospital."

After what seems to Ray an age, a second ambulance arrives and takes Aubrey to Metropolitan Hospital. The emergency room resident is not encouraging, saying tersely, "He has lost too much blood."

New Child finds out what has happened later, after the movie. "I found out about it when I came home from the movies. Me and my man Bones was sitting on the bench in

Jonathan Projects and he was cracking a Philly cigar to take off the wrapper to put weed in it. So we was sitting there, and we was talking about the movie. It was like I didn't get a funny feeling until I got to the movie theater. It was like I didn't feel right, and everybody was like, 'Yo, what's wrong with you?' I was just sitting there like . . . and we was all getting high."

New Child, Ray, and their mother are keeping vigil at the hospital. Aubrey is still alive in his second day after being shot. He is in a coma and bleeds periodically from his nose and mouth. The hole in his face is covered with bandages. New Child tends to him, from time to time wiping blood from his face.

"It's like Ray was talking to Aubrey and laughing with him, and the next thing you know he laying there on the ground, bleeding out of his face and his head. And right after it happened, Ray kept saying, 'It happened so fast. It happened so fast.' It really affected him. Me and Aubrey was always tight. Ray and Aubrey were starting to get real tight."

New Child is at the hospital talking to a friend named Smoky, who tells him that he had been shot twice in the head and lived after being in a coma for six months. Smoky, twenty-four, is at the hospital to help in any way that he can.

"One of Smoky's partners was jealous of him and set him up is basically what happened. He told somebody where he was going to be at, and he was on line at a club, and they came and shot him."

Smoky says to New Child in Aubrey's room, "Talk to him. Wally, talk to him. Trust me, because even though I couldn't move, I could hear people. I could hear when people in my family talked. I just couldn't respond."

So New Child talks to Aubrey: "I wish I was there, this

wouldn't have happened. You a big, strong brother. Don't die on me. You used to tell me, 'Be strong, Wally. Be strong,' so you got to be strong for me and for everybody." New Child is rubbing Aubrey's chest and "I was talking to him and he just grabbed my hand like this, and he just gave me that shake like, 'Don't worry about me.' It was bugged, but that's how I took it, like he was like, 'Little brother, don't worry about me.' "

Two days later Aubrey is dead.

"My brother didn't deserve that. He wasn't nobody out there robbing nobody, sticking nobody up, abusing women, none of that. He was one of the most respectful people you want to meet. I think I got my humbleness from him, like knowing how to be grateful for the little things in life, I got that from him."

Within days, Julio is arrested. Julio quickly informs on the African-American boy, the shooter, who is arrested, tried, and convicted. The judge sentences him to eight and one-third to twenty-five years in prison. To date, he has served ten. Julio does not serve time.

"They said in court that they planned on shooting somebody that night. They said that the brother that shot my brother, he was the one that really wanted to do it. But they was all in ca-hoots, like, 'Yo, tonight we going to shoot somebody. We going to catch a body.' That's how they was doing. As silly as it seems, that's how they was thinking.

"I think it starts in their house, their household. If their mother never really hugs them and shows them love or their father always beating on them and stuff like that, it makes them cold. They get numb to certain things.

"We not born like that. We conditioned. We taught. Even if your parents don't say, 'You know what? Hate yourself and hate other people and shoot at other people and hurt other people.' I don't think no parents tell their kids that, but you can indirectly tell them that by how you treat them. If you treat your kid a certain way and they love you and all that and you don't give them no love, they going to have that in them when they hit the streets that, 'Man, my parents don't love me, so F everybody. I don't care about nothing, nobody.' "

A month after Aubrey's death, his father calls. New Child answers the telephone. He does not know how long it has been since he last heard his father's voice, years maybe.

Father: "Hello. Is this Wallace?"

New Child: "Yes."

Father: "This is your father." Pause. "How is your mom?"

New Child: "She's hanging in there."

Father: "How's . . . ?" Long pause. New Child is silent. He wants his father to say the name, the name of his firstborn child, his namesake. But his father, who has changed his own name to an Islamic name, seems either not to remember his firstborn child's name or . . . what? "H-how's Aubrey?"

New Child: "Aubrey is dead."

Father: Long silence. "What do you mean?"

New Child: "What do you think I mean? He got killed. He got killed a month ago."

Father: "What happened?" New Child tells him.

"He didn't cry or nothing. He was just like, 'Damn, my oldest son.' I didn't even want to talk to him, because it was like his reaction, it wasn't real, because he was detached from us. He wasn't grief-stricken. It was like he was trying to feel it, but he couldn't feel it. And I didn't even want to talk to him no more. I think I gave the phone to my mother or something. But, I wasn't even really mad at him, because I felt, like, man, if he knew better, he'd do better. That's how I felt."

New Child is angry. Angry at the world. Aubrey's death has stoked this anger white-hot. With respect to his father's desertion, New Child is more damaged than angry. In any case, he has never been stigmatized by it. Of three hundred or so kids he knows, he can identify only twenty fathers who are active participants in their children's lives.

"I look at it like the things that may have been flawed as far as my father's concerned, and even my mother from seeing it for so many years and watching it, with the help of God I'll be able to avoid it and not do certain things that they have done, especially abandon my children. That's one thing I vowed never to do.

"I told my mother, I said, 'If I was ever to get married and it didn't work out and I had children, even if I didn't like the woman anymore, couldn't stand to see her,' I said, 'I wouldn't take that out on my children, because they don't have nothing to do with it.' "

In the days, weeks, and months following Aubrey's death, New Child goes completely out of control. He begins to drink—vodka, gin, cognac—anything he can get his hands on. Beer is his staple. Olde English. He drinks it like morning juice, guzzling down as much as a quart at the top of the day. "I was an alcoholic at sixteen." He sits in class either drunk or weeded out of his skull. He stays out all night. He rebels against all authority: "cops, teachers, anybody." He questions the existence of God.

19

PEEWEE AND NEW CHILD: SAVING THEMSELVES AND SAVING OTHERS

New Child met Peewee the summer of 1992, the summer after Aubrey was murdered. In that first meeting, he told Peewee what had happened to his brother. After their second meeting he told him that he wanted to kill everybody who had any connection with Aubrey's death. The first exchange had happened after New Child had run into his man Boonie Rock in front of the Johnson Projects on Lexington where New Child's grandmother lived.

Boonie had come up to New Child and said, "Yo, Y-Z and some dude that's trying to manage artists, they up there at Big Bill's house. They want us to come up there and rhyme." That's how New Child met Peewee.

"I went up to Big Bill's house. Brother Y-Z, the rapper, and Peewee was talking. And I was like, 'Yo, who's this dude?' He was different. He was real different to me. I was like, 'Yo, who is this brother?' I was just watching him."

Peewee turned and asked New Child, "What's up with you? You rhyme?"

"Yes," New Child answered.

"Well, let me hear something. Why you sitting in the

corner all quiet?" New Child rhymed something and Peewee said, "All right, that's read, but can you rhyme off your head?"

New Child started to rhyme extemporaneously. Peewee said, "Yo, you got a gift."

New Child said, "Listen, if I don't do this rap thing, I don't got no life." Peewee looked at him quizzically and was silent for a moment. Then he said, "Is that right?" Only mildly incredulous.

"Yes," New Child answered, more emphatically this time. "If I don't do this rap, I don't have no life. I already know it. I'm going to be where my brother's at."

"What happened to your brother?"

"My brother got killed a year ago."

"What?"

"Yes."

A week later, New Child and Boonie met with Peewee and Kleopatra, Peewee's wife, at the Milbank Center in Harlem on 118th Street between Fifth and Lenox. After New Child rhymed for a while, Peewee signed him to a management contract.

New Child says, "He seemed real and sincere. But I still didn't trust him. I would talk to him over the phone and we would talk about things. Our relationship got deeper than just manager-artist. It was like father-son, because he seen the things that I was going through, like I was getting arrested all the time, and I would call him, and he'd talk about it, and he'd drop some jewels [advice] on me. He'd say, 'Child, nothing's going to change in your life until you change it.' The kid that killed my brother, he was locked up, so I couldn't get him, but I wanted to get his peoples, and I was going to get his peoples. Peewee said to me, 'Child, whatever you do, it's not going to bring your brother back. No matter how many of them you kill, it ain't going to bring him back."

Not long ago, I sat down with New Child in New York. I wanted to know what qualified Peewee for his trust. What gave him and not someone else a language that New Child and others like him could understand and listen to?

"Nobody else could reach me besides somebody like Peewee. I was too far gone, and Peewee, I could relate to his struggle when he told me what he went through, and it wasn't like somebody just trying to tell me to stop, and he was saying, 'Child, I did so much time in jail. I seen so many of my friends die. I was away from my family too long.' We identified with each other. So, that was the first step: identification. I just said, 'Whoa.' "

Every Sunday in New York, Peewee Kirkland holds his School of Skillz. Beleaguered black mothers bring the young black boys upon whom American society makes undeclared war every day. They come from homes held together by women who are alone and spent beneath their burden. They attend schools that are little more than inmate factories to produce the fodder to fuel the economy of the new American slavery. They are the coveted prey of a new elite of prison-state industrialists. They are ancient Abyssinia's modern American offspring whose only allowed manhood finds expression in the career of the thug. They are the legatees of the old slavery and the prime candidates for the new. They are as young as eight, nine, ten years of age. They are the man-children, lost and angry—and armed. They are post-Christian America's state-trained gladiators who slaughter each other before empty seats, the losers dying, the winners filling the state-built iron plantations that ballast the new economy of increasingly skewed privilege. They are the rapidly expanding class of Americans whose plight professional *leaders*, black and white, have all but ignored.

They come every Sunday with their mothers and they talk. They talk to Peewee and to New Child and to each other. They listen only to these, the authentic, trustworthy voices, voices found on their streets, found in their art, the starkly honest literature of rap music.

A little boy, ten years old, dressed in blue, is stopped by New Child.

"Yo, what's all that blue about?"

"HG, man, HG, HG."

"What's HG?"

"Harlem Gangsters, man. I'm a gangster." The boy smiles so broadly, his cheeks are near to popping. The face innocent yet.

"Stop laughing and tell me what you think a gangster is," says New Child. The boy hesitates, and New Child says with a serious smile, "You ain't no gangster. Come here and let me talk to you."

New Child Lynch does, and the ten-year-old boy listens.

AFTERWORD

Many would ask how Peewee Kirkland had saved the life of New Child Lynch and how he continues to salvage wayward youth through his Sunday School of Skillz sessions. Peewee, trusted and credible, is successful because he cares deeply about those to whom America has denied all social opportunity and turned a calloused back for an unbroken age. Himself a victim, Peewee has tried to shoulder a responsibility that a culpable official America has progressively abjured. As weary as Sisyphus and bereft of resources, Peewee has altered the course of countless lives with a fatherlike love and simple caring.

Young black people do not *want* to destroy themselves. Given a constructive alternative, they would not elect to lead a life of crime that would ultimately land them in prison, or worse. But millions of black youth have discerned that official America does not care what happens to them. It did not care in the age of American slavery. It did not care in the age of Jim Crow discrimination and, at home and abroad, it does not care now. (It has recently come to light that Clinton administration officials knew well in advance that Hutu militias in Rwanda

269

were organizing the 1994 genocide that would claim up to a half-million African lives. Yet Bill Clinton, the president upon whom African-Americans lavish unbridled affection, did nothing. He did not even care enough to call a single high-level meeting to discuss measures that might have been taken by the United States to prevent the slaughter.)

Thus, it should occur broadly at least to African-Americans, that nothing can happen to slow our society's descent to an envisioned America of 2076, unless African-Americans themselves take initiatives to help the millions of our young now caught in the crosshair of American official indifference.

At Peewee Kirkland's request, I have changed the names of all represented in his and New Child Lynch's stories except their own and those of the members of their immediate families. The events that Peewee and New Child described to me in a series of taped interviews actually occurred. I have taken a measure of literary license in order to disguise the identities of those who played a role in their compelling stories, while at the same time giving accurately the race, gender, and ethnicity of these role players. Where necessary, I have invented dialogue, family circumstance, and personas for the renamed role players inasmuch as I could not learn the internal details of their lives.

News stories and letters to the editor appear in this book as they appeared in the *New York Times* and *Washington Post*. With the exception, of course, of the names and events envisioned for 2076 and the people represented in Peewee's and New Child's accounts, I have used real names from real news accounts.

Lastly, Mark Lawrence's and Furious Stylze's names are real, as are, in general, places, institutions, events, occurrences, and people described in the text.

MY PLEA

Why haven't you learned anything?
Man that school . . . is a joke
The same people control the school system control
The prison system, and the whole system
Ever since slavery, nawsayin'?

—FROM THE SONG "THEY SCHOOLS"
BY THE RAP GROUP DEAD PREZ

I make this appeal to fellow African-Americans. White Americans may read it. That is fine. But it is not addressed to them.

All of the socioeconomic data confirm that we trail the American mainstream in every area of critical measure. This should surprise no one. No people could endure what we alone have endured in America for more than three and a half centuries and not suffer badly for it.

Over the last three years, I have been centrally involved in the reparations movement seeking restitution to the contemporary descendents of American slaves for economic and social disadvantages born of slavery and the century of government-based

271

racial discrimination that followed in its train. I am confident of ultimate success. But that is not the point of this appeal.

Were we to receive $10 trillion tomorrow and we had not ourselves taken collateral measures to repair the psychological injury that we have sustained during the long, unremitting on-slaught, the money would do us no lasting benefit. After a decades-long campaign waged in a court of global opinion, we may well receive for our pains a measure of material recom-pense. But little else in the way of comfort should be hoped for from a nation that perpetrated against us the longest-running crime against humanity known to the world over the last five hundred years. In any case, money alone cannot heal us. The healing of our spirits we must do for ourselves. Until we can manage to do this for a critical mass of those of us who have been most put-upon, we will not be able to salvage ourselves as a race in America.

The whole point of slavery was to convert uncompensated black labor into a sustainable tradition of white wealth and privilege. And then, of course, there were ancillary objectives, one of which, long observed, was the success of those who would make some of us enemies against others of us, no matter how unwitting. No form of slavery, ante- or postbellum (today's urban form), can endure without a measure of cooperation from its victims.

On November 9, 1862, Sarah Morgan, a member of a Ba-ton Rouge, Louisiana, slaveholding family, wrote in her diary:

"Last night we girls [Sarah and her sister] sat on the wood just in front of the furnace—twenty [slaves] of all ages crowded around, we sang away to their great amusement. Poor op-pressed devils! Why did you not chunk us with the burning logs instead of looking happy, and laughing like fools? Really some good old abolitionist is needed here, to tell them how miserable they are. Can't mass Abe spare a few to enlighten his brethren?"

Sarah and the twenty slaves have modern counterparts whose relationship to each other could aptly be described with much the same language that Sarah Morgan used in her diary nearly 140 years ago.

Grinding poverty, wretched schools, dysfunctional families, and a general self-regard of angry hopelessness are killing our young people and driving a burgeoning national prison economy, and again largely for the benefit of private, white economic interests. But, *we* collaborate. We collaborate with the relative silence of black professional leadership. We collaborate when a president builds prisons, willy-nilly, to house *us*, and we support *him* uncritically, anyhow. For if Bill Clinton must be today's Sarah, so must silent blacks be today's twenty slaves *looking happy and laughing like fools.*

Young urban blacks are being destroyed in our streets, schools, and jails in alarming numbers. Yet little more than a whimper has issued from black *leaders*. We lament racial profiling, as indeed, we should. But, we appear to do this without understanding that racial profiling is the tree, not the forest. Perhaps we have misfocused so badly because of considerations driven by class. Racial profiling affects *all* blacks. The warehousing of poor blacks in prisons affects only *them*, as if Peewee's and New Child's fate were not indissolubly bound up with all the rest of ours.

And while we are at it, let us demystify any pride taken in the relative material and social success of some of us vis-à-vis the painful lot of a frighteningly growing number of the rest of us. During the long centuries of slavery, some of our men, women, and children were brutalized by their masters beyond belief. Others, though badly treated, managed to keep at least their spirits, their core psyches, intact. I suspect that those of us, upon emancipation, who enjoyed that psychological advantage were those whose descendents have managed to escape the urban hells that trap so many of our young now.

I have a picture on my dining room wall taken of my family in North Carolina in the 1870s. Seen in the picture are my great-great-grandparents flanked by my great-grandfather, his six sisters, and two brothers, all dressed for church and wearing stern visages. They were born in slavery. They were not well-off but they were not destitute. More importantly, it is clear from their bearing that though they had suffered, their spirits had not been broken. They were possessed of obvious social values and standards. I am a linear beneficiary of their relative social stability. Peewee and New Child cannot trace their family lines as I can mine. They had not the benefit of rock-solid intergenerational families. Their survival is a miracle. Mine is not.

But miracles occur infrequently. Bad social conditions almost always produce bad results. All across America, little-known, underfunded, idealistic blacks like Peewee and New Child are waging human salvage battles in urban hellholes. They are doing this with little to no support from mainline black leadership. We, especially those of us who've been fortunate enough to reach higher ground, must help them. We must look into our hearts and reach into our pockets and give to their programs. We must raise the profile of their struggle. We must make our leaders lead. We must contribute our talents. We must listen, without prejudice, to the urban poets of rap protest. We must connect their struggle, our struggle, to the travails of another time and understand, at last, the logic of causality.

In many ways, the children of the urban hip-hop generation have been victimized by the success of the civil rights movement, inasmuch as *integration* provided tickets to some of us doctors, teachers, lawyers, et al., to leave the rest of us. As a child, all of my role models were black people whom my family knew. They made house calls. They graded our papers. They represented us at the bar. They extended a family that was already sturdy. The very best talent that our community had to offer served our community alone, in part because segregation left them little choice. I was poor. But in no social sense was I aware of it. It must be said that this social safety net self-provided by the black community in the worst of times was not universally available. Peewee was growing up in Harlem when I was growing up in Richmond, Virginia. There was no net in the Harlem fifties strong enough to save him from grief. Nonetheless, the Harlem of those years is hardly the Harlem of today where the thug-life virus has become epidemic.

The civil rights movement alarmed white liberal sensibilities enough to allow blacks a certain opportunity of movement, access, and limited success. But white society has never seriously concerned itself with the eradication of *white* poverty. Hence, it is logical to assume that white society would be even less concerned about the consequences of black poverty.

Then of course, there are questions about the fairness of the American criminal justice system. No one questions that poverty gives rise to criminal activity, at least the criminal activity that is most frequently punished. It is bad enough that national policy makers accept that poverty is a breeding ground for crime and do nothing about the underlying condition. But, this wilful abdication of responsibility becomes, indeed, even more contemptible when the laws punishing such crimes are enforced in a racially discriminatory fashion. As you learned from Manning Marable's fine paper, blacks comprise fourteen percent of the nation's drug users but constitute seventy-five percent of prison admissions for drug offenses. This is just one of many yawning discrepancies in the application of law that cannot be explained away.

I am not suggesting here that the hugely disproportionate incarceration of blacks results from some smoke-filled-room white conspiracy. I *am* suggesting that white national opinion makers have arranged a much too convenient construction of an American conscience that manages to ignore how criminals are developed, apprehended, charged, convicted, and punished.

Given all that has happened, shouldn't we all be instantly suspicious whenever a tide of black captives creates profits for white investors, jobs for white towns, and talking points for white demagogues? But no one will raise the hue and cry until blacks do, and from every corner of our community. For, what is at stake here is our very future as a people in America.

INDEX

ACKNOWLEDGMENTS

I should like first to thank Mark Lawrence whose invitations to speak inspired the writing of this book. I wish also to thank Peewee Kirkland, New Child Lynch, and Furious Stylze not only for their trust but further for their friendship. I am deeply grateful to Pauline Barfield for allowing me the use of her New York offices in which the discussions that gave rise to this work were held. I am further in debt to Professor Manning Marable whose seminal scholarship on the American criminal justice system I cite copiously. Mention must also be made of my literary agent, Marie Brown, without whose support I'd likely never have gotten around to writing books in the first place. I would also like to thank my editor Brian Tart whose suggestions were useful and appreciated. Thanks as well to Margaret Dodo who typed the manuscript with great patience. Lastly, I thank my wife, Hazel, without whose support, advice, and wisdom, I am but half a man.

Randall Robinson is the founder and president of TransAfrica, the organization that has spearheaded the movement for influencing U.S. politics toward international black leadership. Frequently featured in major print media, he has appeared on *The Charlie Rose Show*, *Today*, *Good Morning America*, *20/20*, *60 Minutes*, *The Tom Joyner Show*, and BET, among others.